Fifty-Five Positive Steps Black People Can Take to Preserve Themselves Into the 21st Century

Fifty-Five Positive Steps Black People Can Take to Preserve Themselves Into the 21st Century

Michael W. Cromwell

iUniverse, Inc.
New York Lincoln Shanghai

Fifty-Five Positive Steps Black People Can Take to Preserve Themselves Into the 21st Century

iUniverse, Inc.

For information address:
iUniverse, Inc.
2021 Pine Lake Road, Suite 100
Lincoln, NE 68512
www.iuniverse.com

ISBN: 0-595-31439-2

Printed in the United States of America

Contents

Preface

I wrote this because I care about black people—my people. Like Dr. King did, I have a dream as well. I would like to see, if possible in my lifetime, a greater unity among American blacks. I'd like to see a greater sense of community among those of my own kind. Such unity did at one time exist. But it disintegrated quickly following integration in the 1960s. But I for one would love to see a more cohesive black community come into existence in an integrated America. Simply put, there is strength in numbers. This is not a cliché. By coming together more, we, as black people, can help ourselves and help each other. As it stands now, we all, to large degrees, operate as independent islands and try to find our ways in the world mostly alone.

What saddens me as an African-American is that I think there is a will to be more united among blacks, but an ignorance and in some cases, a fear, of attempting to do so. I feel this longing; I sense it. Why can't such unity happen? What could make it take place?

What I have proposed below in the form of a list, is a guide to certain areas where black Americans can shore of their lives in the areas of self-esteem, spiritual development, personal confidence, and communal unity, among other areas. I put my advice in the form of a list because, frankly, this is a way that our society has come to like to process information. It is easy and "comfortable" to the reading and intellectual mind. In addition, the entries on my list are randomized, designed this way on purpose to keep the reader off balance intentionally, so that he or she will not have time to mull over each entry right away, but only upon some, hopefully, serious reflection. Each subsequent entry then comes in on another completely different topic that will also hopefully spur some reflection before moving on to the following entry. Any entry might apply to a particular area in the life of a given black American. I attempted to cover areas I have noticed that I have had to address in my life over the years and things I have noticed in other black people out there in the world—to include black children and youth—and extrapolated meanings. Indulge me, if you will. What do you have to lose?

Finally, in case you are a non-black reader and have wondered, any advice given here is also offered to you and your own kind. I target my own people for personal reasons. Please do not begrudge me my desire to relate to my own. Here I would have to draw the line. But the white, the Hispanic, the Indian and the Asian is of course more than welcome to peruse what I have written here, as what I have to say, I believe applies to all.

One more thing to black people: Consider while you read, before you read, and hopefully after you do, to unite as a people in your hearts, minds and souls. Consider the benefits and the challenges. Consider the hopes, dreams and aspirations of the more optimistic of our ancestors for a stable future black progeny, stable because they are comfortable with themselves in a just society. We achieved justice when we were united. Remember? To maintain this may require an even stronger unification.

God bless you and be with you of course.

Sincerely,

Mike Cromwell

55. Forgive Yourself

This can be easier said than done. How many of us prevent ourselves from advancing because of some past gripe with ourselves or past woe that we cannot overcome. We cannot forget about the past completely, but we cannot allow it to prevent us from living in the present and planning for our futures. To do so would essentially be to stop living altogether. Forgive yourself, and move on.

Of course there are degrees of crime and sin that some of us must overcome that are worse than others. But none of us can go back and change the past. We can only live in the present where hopefully we can live to correct the wrongs of the past. However, the first step is to forgive oneself and, in the future, to avoid the behavior that may have led you to such guilt. Learn from your mistakes, in other words, and move on.

54. Forgive Others

This is also easier said than done. I realize this. Holding a grudge always seems easier. We can feed off a grudges in some strange ways. The problem is that many people do not know how to forgive. And how do we do it?

Most importantly, the type and degree of offense should not matter. Forgiveness should transcend such considerations. Should I be angrier and less likely to forgive the person who does harm to a loved one than the person who knocks me over on the bus or cuts me off in traffic? Most likely, for the reality is that the degree of the offense usually does, in fact, determine our ability and willingness to forgive. The worse the offense, the longer we are to hold a grudge and less likely to forgive.

However the key is, and the point to be imposed here, is that the mechanism in the heart that allows us to forgive in the first place should not discriminate between the nature of the offense. In other words, if we are able to develop in our hearts the ability to forgive for one offense, this same spirit should cover all of them. The question then is how do we develop such a spirit. The answer is that we must learn to open up our own hearts and learn to understand the hearts of our "offenders," realize that these people are human beings like we are and prone to misunderstanding, fear, hate, doubt and all the others. We can start learning to forgive others when we learn to see our own selves in the people who offend us or have offended us. We are capable of negative emotions, and so are they. Neither they nor us are perfect. When this understanding is assumed, then whether we forgive or not becomes a matter of choice. My encouragement here would be to forgive others in all occasions and circumstances, as carrying grudges and burdens is like carrying hatred and other negative emotions around with us. To relieve ourselves of such negative emotions can then free up our minds and feelings to more positive ones that we can empty into ourselves, empty out to loved ones and to the world at large to make it a better place.

Expunge the bad; replace it with the good and consistently transmit that good to others.

53. Learn And Understand Humility

What is it? Humility? Many of us today would have to secure a dictionary to come up with a definition. Without such a guide, many would say the word means something like "being nice and kind to others" or perhaps the state of being generally "quiet and soft spoken." These descriptions are close and much better than describing humility as the "the degree of moisture in the atmosphere." No, humility is not humidity. Not even close. In fact, I will define it for you here. Humility is "the state of being humble." What then does it mean to be humble? It means not being "proud or haughty, arrogant or assertive;" "unpretentious, offered in a spirit of deference or submission." These are the direct dictionary definitions of the word.

Some people are humble by nature, perhaps introverted. Then there are those who are extroverted and have a need to be seen and heard. But there can always be a balance. The key is to know when to humble oneself. This usually revolves around the occasion. We are humble at funerals, for example, out of respect. And respect is the key. We should know when and where to show the proper respect. Especially our young. But who deserves respect? People in authority such as teachers and parents deserve respect. Also, the elderly. A sense of respect often comes before humility.

As individuals, we need to practice humility as a calming influence on our spirits. Such activity might succeed in lowering our blood pressures more than medication. If we give of ourselves, our natural desires to be prideful and assertive and haughty and all the rest, we will be left with respect, peace, patience and personal dignity. Contrary to popular belief, when we are humble, we are winners, not losers.

52. Respect Yourself

In the black community, this mantra has been repeated for decades. "Respect Yourself." It gained its most ground in the 1960s during the civil rights work of both Dr. Martin Luther King Jr. and Malcolm X. "Respect Yourself." And it was uttered to black people as a verbal esteem booster. The power of the declaration has not waned over the years. Black people still need to respect themselves in all areas of life: dress and appearance, attitude, and thinking. What comes to mind most immediately today are images of young black men wearing their pants down past their waists, a fad that many in the older generation cannot seem to comprehend. For the older guys, such behavior by their sons smacks immediately of a kind of self-esteem problem, a lack of care for how they look and therefore who they are and what they want to represent. The denigration of women and self in popular music also smacks hard of a lack of self-respect and so would something like black-on-black crime. It can be argued that we kill ourselves because we do not like or respect ourselves.

However, the goal for old and young alike is to respect yourself and be proud of yourself, your life and accomplishments, whatever they might be. Meanwhile, don't take anything for granted and be humbly thankful for everything you have.

51. Love Yourself

This follows naturally. How can we respect ourselves if we first do not love ourselves? Loving ourselves is the key, the crux, and the heart of the regeneration of the American black community. And the key in loving oneself is in loving oneself despite how we perceive the way the world wants us to see ourselves. Ignore the world. Ignore trends, fads and advertising if they are not for you. Love yourself first and then work from there. Find reasons to love yourself. Discover your uniqueness. I do not speak of vanity and narcissism, standing in the mirror for several hours and admiring yourself. I speak of getting to know ourselves and then trusting who we are in good times and bad. Trust your opinions, thoughts and beliefs and don't be afraid to share them. Loving yourself will give you the confidence to do so.

Do you love you? You need to learn. It might help to imagine yourself as someone else and that you are looking at yourself from outside your body, seeing yourself as an objective observer. Who is this person? Is he or she likeable? Why? Why not? You will come up with something. You must. But, in your evaluation, reject how you believe the world sees you and love yourself despite the world. In your evaluation of yourself you must ignore the world.

50. Acquire A "World View"

There is the "I," which is referred to in the previous steps. Then there is the "all" of which "we" are a part of, born into. There is a universe; there are galaxies within that universe; solar systems within those galaxies; planets within them, revolving around stars that give the planets life. Our star is called the sun and it sustains us. On our planet, which has existed anywhere from 20 billion to just over 6,000 years, depending on one's "world view," there are at present approximately 6 billion of us, to go along with perhaps at least as many varied animal, bird and fish species. Nearly a third of the world's population exists within the borders of two countries alone: India and China. The United States has roughly 300 million people, of which about 12 to 15 percent are of African descent, like you. Hispanics, however, have surpassed blacks as the nation's largest "minority." The continent of Europe is now evolving into one giant super state, to rival our United States; the conflict between Israel and the Palestinians has existed since 1948 when the state of Israel became a modern nation. To buffer the European Union, the Asian nations, including China and Japan, might one day unite themselves to form a "super" bloc of countries. This last item of information is speculation. The others are facts and in one week's time, any one of us, through the multiplicity of media outlets, can achieve knowledge involving the above. Detailed knowledge, however, can only be found in history books.

The point is that we as black people would serve ourselves well to become better informed, at least when it comes to the chief issues of the day, the ones we hear so much about. Knowledge of the issues can help us to become more viable and perhaps more successful members of society. We need to learn to think beyond the here and now and think about the future, as well as the past, and we need to go the extra mile in the sense that when we decide to investigate an issue, we need to learn the history of it. Do not take the media characterization of events for granted. For example, with regard to the Israeli-Palestinian conflict in the Middle East, don't just take the media's word for it. Research the history of it yourself and try to evaluate both sides fairly. In general, acquire a "world view" based on your knowledge of the universe, the world and history, and you do not necessarily need to possess a college education to acquire a world view.

With regard to the new information society and our places in the universe, black people have lived in the dark for too long. It's time for us to get into the conversation, to get into the game, to let people know that we have opinions on things that they don't expect us to have opinions on. Watch the "News Hour with Jim Lehrer" on PBS one afternoon, for example, and try to figure out what is going on and what is being said.

Finally, the mission with which I charge you is to discover the black American's place in the context of world history. Because I assure you that our significance extends well beyond that of some enslaved aberration.

49. Trust Other Black People

There is little trust in our society today. You see it on the bus, in the streets, sometimes in the workplace and, sorry to say, even within families. With regard to trust, we are reaching rock bottom, perhaps in the history of civilization itself. There is suspicion and the threat of violence at every corner, it seems. Much of this new behavior has to do with mistrust.

There was a time when black people trusted one another more. That was before integration. After integration there has been a fracturing in our community that has exploded in recent years. Now, fully immersed in the culture at large—a culture becoming more diverse and competitive each day—the impulse is to free ourselves from old ties and make ourselves as lighter and freer to pursue those things we think will give us happiness, either material or emotional. Sacrificed in the "pursuit of the self"—a 1990s critical mass of the 1970s "me" generation—are family, relationships (specifically those between men and women in the black community) and black personal relationships in general. As blacks, our collective ship has crashed on what has turned out to be the rocky shores of integration, leaving us all orphans scurrying for the largest pieces of driftwood we can find and, generally speaking, unwilling to pool our resources to help one another survive. It's every man and woman for him and her self, a kind of philosophy that not did exist in our community prior to the 1960s. We have become selfish, vain and greedy, taking from the society established by the "majority" culture the worst possible elemental vestiges.

At the barber shop recently (such locations remain hotbeds of peculiar street wisdom) I walked into the very middle of a conversation between my barber and his man in the chair where they were discussing the seeming disdain that blacks have for other blacks in the street. Specifically, they were referring to the blacks downtown who had "made it" but were apparently unwilling to share their success with even a look in the eye to a fellow black, much less a kind word or a smile. The speculation by the barber and his customer, their conclusion, was that, those "made it" blacks were too ashamed of "something" to share with those of their kind, perhaps because they were too concerned and stressed over their own struggles and did not want to be dragged down and exposed by one of their own kind. In any case, the barber and his friend remarked that despite their outward appearances, these "made it" blacks did not look happy; in fact, they appeared just the opposite: they looked grim and depressed. Before concluding this topic in their conversation and moving on to a next, the guy in the chair remarked that such fear, loathing and self-loathing among blacks was not reduced to the haves and have not in the community, but among blacks of modest means. The fact is that there is no sense of community at all, and that you run the risk of not getting a hello out of a black grandmother in the supermarket checkout line (something you might once have taken for granted) as you would from one of your peers, or even an adolescent. Yes, blacks too—excuse me, African Americans—have fallen into the same trap of mean spiritedness that has gripped the rest of this nation, though perhaps not to the extent that other racial groups have. And this has always been our peculiar gift: to rise out of darkness and suffering, like the Phoenix, to sing and create. Therefore, I issue a challenge to you here my fellow black brothers and sisters! Unite! Come together again! Do not be afraid of who is watching you or what they think! Do not be afraid to speak to one other in the halls and at the water coolers! Fight for your rights to socialize and commune together! And not just for sex, but socially! There is strength in numbers! One day we might have to discover this fact the hard way when all of our backs are pressed against the wall and we might be forced come together, so we may as well start getting to know one another, all over again. The fact is that we have never forgotten each other. To this day we know each other very well. We are just afraid to talk to each other about what is on our minds and in our hearts. Learn to look one another in the eye and then to trust those of your kind with what's in your heart.

48. Stay Fit

To stay fit, we must first get fit. Such an idea would never have occurred to me had I not served several years in the U.S. Army where fitness was a mandatory and career requirement. Not staying fit and being able to pass the required fitness tests could get you kicked out of the military. There is certainly a discipline to staying fit. For most civilians, it might boil down to a routine. But the rewards of fitness—top fitness—are great. Indeed, achieving muscle tone and cardiovascular conditioning can alter one's complete perspective on life. Food might taste better, sight clearer, endurance, stamina, attention span, all these things are enhanced when the body is in top condition. You might perform better at work, have more energy to spend with children, read with greater accuracy, become a more alert driver—all these areas can be affected by cutting off body fat and enhancing breathing capacity through fitness. Top fitness is then, not a joke, and should not be underrated. It can amount to a key life advantage if achieved and maintained. For blacks in particular, the benefits of fitness would undoubtedly help to combat some health conditions almost exclusive to our community, to include diabetes, strokes, cardiovascular disease and high blood pressure.

Perhaps a common fallacy is that people who are not "visibly" overweight, might believe that they are in good shape. This might not necessarily be the case. There is always room for improvement. For those who "are" visibly overweight, possessing neither endurance nor stamina and for whom their extra pounds are a life burden, these people might need to seriously evaluate their lifestyles. No, weight loss is not easy and I succeeded in getting in shape, in large part, because the

Army made me. But I survived the army's rigors to pass on the value of staying fit along to you.

Lastly, I, here, promote fitness through exercise and not through extreme diets and surgeries and while some of you out there might think that you are fine the way that you are, I submit to you that you might even become better and perform better, achieving that extra edge needed to compete, through the hard and disciplined work of routine exercise. A half an hour to 45 minutes a day will work, with alternating routines of cardio work and weights would be an initial recommendation given here. But please, consult a doctor before engaging in any exercise program.

47. Reduce Television Time

Television is a brain drainer. All of the visual media are, in fact, because there is very little interaction, just the watching and, afterwards, the forming of superficial opinions that do little to influence our overall common good. With regard to the visual media, we are both victims and subjects. Television sucks the very life right out of us and while I will not in this particular segment advocate the reading of books—this will come later—instead, I will advocate getting to know people. Instead of watching fictional people through the fictional media of television, I will advocate going out and meeting and dealing with the real things, the people that walk the streets, those individuals in possession of souls, the people we hurriedly pass by on the way home to watch our favorite television shows, those people called human beings. We need to get to know each other. Black people do, certainly, as I have already stated above; meanwhile, with regard to television watching, countless studies have been conducted showing that blacks watch more television than any other racial group, pinning us in our beds and to our sofas, a kind of self-imposed brainwashing. For blacks in particular, TV can be ranked up there with drugs and alcohol as those elements of society that we have allowed to bring us down as a people. For black people, television has led to inaction and, perhaps, unrealistic perceptions of reality.

I am not saying that we should stop watching television altogether, just do it, and you knew I was going to say it, in moderation. In return for the six or seven hours we reject of television in a given week, use that time to establish or re-establish family bonds, go out and do something fun with your wife, play with you kids somewhere outdoors, go somewhere and watch "real" people come and go—perhaps with a friend—and enjoy it; join a club that is involved in something that you have always wanted to do, or introduce yourself to someone who you have always been curious about. (For this last one, remember to be "humble" when you go up to a strange person. Don't let your pride be hurt if you are rejected and please try, try again, if you are so inclined. People are more sensitive these days).

But get away from the TV or any visual apparatus from time to time and get to know the real things—real people.

46. Eat Healthier

Along with exercise, the benefits of eating well cannot be overstated. What I have learned is that we pretty much know what is good for us and what is not before we even take the first bite. The solution is in what we choose to eat, when, how much of it and how often. We cannot, for example, eat fast food meals more than once a day. Fast food restaurants exist; they have been around for generations, they taste good and they are not going to go away. But this does not mean that we have to abuse them. Instead, we should treat their products as occasional treats. Perhaps a Big Mac and fries, for example, one day a week as a treat. The trick is to know when to stop. In between such snacks, there should be "right" and "balanced" eating, to include fruit, vegetables and the consumption of adequate amounts of water along with other beverages. The consumption of water also cannot be overstated.

Meanwhile, exercise should always be in the mix. The combination of eating right and exercise can lead to stronger minds and stronger bodies. But please, consult a physician before engaging in any exercise regimen or diet plan. Any such undertakings will depend on age, body type, health history and temperament. Find out, through a doctor or exercise counselor or trainer, what works for you. Discover the regimen and eating schedule and stick to them. These are the keys: persistency and consistence after you learn what you have to do.

45. Laugh More

Not only should we laugh more, but we should not be afraid to laugh in the first place. Don't let anyone stifle your desire to laugh and what you may want to laugh at. We all live in a very politically conscious, socially sensitive world now where what we laugh at is scrutinized almost as much as how we vote. Some things that we used to laugh at are now not politically correct targets and not "cool" to laugh at anymore. All that said, you should not feel ashamed of finding humor in the most mundane situations, for the ability to do so can have the effect of getting you through an entire day. Laughter is healthy. And sometimes, we don't even have to laugh out loud; we can quietly laugh and grin to ourselves over some peculiar moment that we might find amusing and there are many such moments to go around each day. (As an aside, it must be noted here, that to laugh *to* yourself, or *at* yourself for that matter, requires the ability to like or love yourself—discussed above—so you must master liking and loving yourself before you can confide in yourself and trust yourself enough to share a laugh with or at yourself.) Many people cannot do this. They cannot confide in themselves enough to share a laugh with themselves. They must share nearly every thought they have with someone else. But do not be afraid to keep some things to yourself and laugh with yourself. Laughter is great medicine. It exercises the lungs, the face muscles, and most importantly, the spirit.

44. Diversify Your Circle Of Friends

As America grows, we, as black people, must grow with it. This does not mean that we must always have to sacrifice our values or beliefs to identify with the culture at large. Just the opposite. Always stay true to yourself. This, other people will respect, whether they be white, Chinese, Indian, Hispanic or Arab. All the races just mentioned are now a part of our daily experiences. Even in remote rural places, ethnic groups of foreign origin are making their presences known—and we as native American blacks have to deal with them and their cultures. We must deal with them at work, in public, and be prepared to be introduced, in some ways, to their cultures, mostly by way of the media. To all this I say that the object is not to be frightened or frustrated with other cultures but to hold our ground. By holding our ground, I reiterate that we should not sacrifice who we are and where we as American blacks have come, as our story and history as a people can rival many of those of other cultures. Not only have we suffered more than most world cultures but we have survived almost fully intact. We must appear to everyone that we meet, no matter where they might be from, as being proud of who we are and where we come from. This does not mean being arrogant, as no other race has the right to feel superior to any other. No, with regard to American blacks, I talk about a noble strength and a resolve in the confidence of our persons and our unique strengths, strengths that have made our black American tribe among the most durable, pluckiest, noblest, most good natured, at times humblest, proudest and most spirited peoples to ever walk the face of the Earth.

After accomplishing the internalization of such pride and such a personal ethic with which to carry out into public to mix with the other races, we can then extend the hand of friendship—this after first defining and becoming comfortable with who we are. Because if we do not know and are not consistent with our own persons, these other races might see through us and try to take advantage of us. This is only human nature. I'm sorry. No, they must be shown to respect us as black men and women. Again, not because of arrogant displays or even intimidation, but through a trade of respect for respect, leading, hopefully to mutual friendship. Once learning how to be friends with people of other races, we would be able to diversify our circle of friends. Such incorporation of new cultures would expand our overall understanding of other cultures and of the world at large and do the same for our new friends. Sure, there will always be those who will not accept the hand of friendship, for their own reasons, but there is never a reason not to try to get to know those outside your own culture and experience. Because whenever the race barrier is ever effectively and legitimately breached, there is always more room to breath for all and always more freedom. Get to know those who do not look like you and entertain the thought and possibility of making them your friends. But first, become solidly grounded in your own identity.

43. Read More

There is only so much we can learn from the visual media, as I have said. In fact, the visual media is very limited. At some point, we have to use our eyes to scan the words on the page of a book, magazine, newspaper or some other branch of the literary medium and read. I know that this strikes fear in some but the advantages can be great. Depending on the mediums you choose to read, you can gain insight into all areas of thought throughout the world, from the Bible on down. In fact, with the Internet now a part of daily life, we are forced to be a more literate culture, as we cannot surf the web without being able to read and read well.

My own reading revolution occurred on a tropical island. Contrary to popular belief, people who can read, read well and get good grades in English language-related work, do not necessarily like to read. This was me before my experience on the island. On the island, Grenada, where I spent almost all of 1992, I found myself homesick. I went there in the early 1990s to try and write some fiction. That ambition notwithstanding, I was still homesick, so I started to buy American newspapers and magazines to see what was going on back in the States. I had access to television—mostly CNN News—but this was not enough. Eventually, even though the American papers and magazines—in particular Newsweek—were expensive, there came a point that I would actually sacrifice food to buy reading material about what was happening back home. Through my desire for information, fueled by homesickness—my reading speed and corresponding comprehension of what I read increased, in my estimation, some six or sevenfold, to the point that I now consider myself to be a borderline speed reader. What my reading abilities have yielded me is the discovery and access into entire new worlds of knowledge through the information I can now pick up through reading just about everything—from advertisements, to warning labels, to operating instructions, to <u>Moby-Dick</u>. The ability to read a variety of literary forms can make an individual very formidable. I would equate it with being able to interpret different dialects and languages within the English language itself and it would behoove all blacks Americans to broaden their reading habits. If you, for example, read your hometown newspaper each day, broaden that to reading a national magazine to see how it might discuss some similar issues of interest to you. Meanwhile, learn how to read the fine print of life, meaning all those areas in advertisement that we all take for granted each day. Understanding advertising in particular and how it targets Americans will enable you to understand yourself through your desires and purchasing trends. When I read Newsweek in Grenada, for example, I would literally read the magazine from cover to cover and sometimes go back and read it again if I could not pay for the next issue. In addition to reading the news in all sections, I would read the ads, large and small, the briefs, and captions in all sections. In this I came to see how a newsmagazine worked and what it produced. My point is that reading is knowledge and knowledge is power and we should not underestimate the value in being able to read, to read well, to understand, to retain and to apply the knowledge we have gained to our lives. The key to reading well is to understand that all of it is interesting—all of it. It is interesting because someone is trying to communicate something to you and to influence you to their purpose and if you read with this understanding in particular, then nothing you read will ever be boring again. The next time you read something, even if it is as simple as an ad, understand that someone might be trying to persuade you to their point of view; and, of course, it will be up to you to decide whether you agree with what is being said or not. But from this moment forward, whenever you read something, whether it is a book or a blurb, instructions on a box or a the writing on dollar bill, ask yourself the following questions: how is this person trying to influence me? What is the basic message trying to be pushed across and is it successful with me? Why or why not?

42. Think More

Except for sleep, there is not a moment in the day when we are not thinking. But the point is that while we are awake and thinking, what are we thinking about, as what we think about as individuals and how we all think, can determine what happens in life. How we live, how we move through life, and, in many ways, where we eventually end up, depends on what and how we think in life.

Most of us, I am assuming, think about how to take care of our most immediate concerns: putting food on the table, rent, children, spouses, family and jobs. These are the fundamental concerns of life that we all have to deal with to various degrees, each and every day we live. Those of us with more latitude—and perhaps more money to spare—might be able to expand such thinking and devote more time than others to areas such as entertainment and recreation, while others of us simply struggle to survive. Still, those fundamental concerns are those which drive us most, rich and poor, large and small, in my estimation and how we harness and sift the thoughts concerning life's necessities regulates our approaches to day to day life. Some of us are more desperate in our thinking, others are level headed and patient realizing that no matter how much we might think about problems, all we can do is our best. In the final analysis, neither approach is necessarily superior to the other. Whether rash or patient all of us have reasons for the things we do and none of us can change the future. What we can do, all of us I believe, is to respect our minds and to exercise them. Do not take them for granted or their potential. My advice here in particular is to stop and think, to literally devote time during the day or within a week to literally think and think only, to reflect on our positions, on those around us who we impact and influence; indeed, spend some time reflecting on your very positions on Earth and in the universe. This all goes back to establishing a worldview. Again, thinking is an exercise and to allow your mind to wander past, present and future and time and space from time to time can work the brain. It can also be very relaxing and soothing. Just because we are black does not mean that we cannot think deeply, even pondering the mysteries of the universe itself. It might behoove us as black people to evade concerns with the here and now, the day to day from time to time and once in a while think such thoughts as: Who am I? Why am I here? How was I created? Is there a God? What makes the Earth spin? What holds the universe together? How large is the universe? Will time end one day? Why will it end? How will it end? How was the universe created and whom was it created for? Who has ownership of it? Why is life so frustrating and why do I think the way that I do? How am I able to think and what is it that animates this body that I inhabit?

As black people, such questions are neither above us nor beneath us and such broad, all encompassing thinking can awaken the mind to new ways of living and approaching daily life.

41. Dream

Don't let reality berate you to the point that you lose your childhood aspirations to dream. Dreaming is fun. You can escape the day to day and relax your mind. You can imagine yourself in other places, with other people, out in space, or doing something you have always wanted to do. Who knows, your dreams might even one day come true. But do not push them away. Invite your dreams in. Welcome them if you feel them taking you over. And I do not speak of sleep dreaming, which none of us can control anyway. I speak of daydreaming, whether voluntary or not. Sometimes we slip into daydreams anyway, especially when we find ourselves bored. But I suggest taking the time to stop and dream on purpose, like thinking on purpose. Like painting a painting, we can draw out our dreams, adding the proper colors and landscapes in our minds. A relaxing process, dreaming can also be a very creative one.

40. Fast

The lesson here is to deny yourself. The overall lesson here is to build strength for yourself and denying yourself will help toward this end. Imagine that thing that you love or love to do most, whether it be eating, watching television, smoking, sleeping in late, or some other activity that pleases your body. Now imagine yourself doing without that behavior for a month; if not a month, then a week; if not a week, then a day. A day sounds much easier to tolerate for the things we love to do most and even might be addicted to in some way. Therefore, my advice is to choose some area of your life that you love and deny yourself doing it for at least a day—to start. If successful, extend this denial of the flesh to a week. I guarantee you that you will become stronger mentally and physically after denying your flesh what you have allowed it to crave for a time.

Generally speaking, fasting is associated with religious practices and religions advise it as a means of self-purification and as an example of devotion to one's faith. With religious backing, fasting might be easier to undertake, therefore, it might help to consult one's religious tradition on the virtues of fasting. However, fasting independently, though difficult, depending on the depth of one's "addiction," can also be done. It takes only some willpower, as does everything else in life that we want to achieve. What you are fighting against with fasting is the body, or the flesh and the flesh is tough to defeat. You will find that as you attempt to fast, other parts of yourself will rebel and you will discover more and more about yourself—what you are able to do and willing to give up in your life and vice versa. You might discover that you are weak, or not as strong as you thought that you were, or that the flesh has more power over you than you thought. Or you might discover that your bodily needs might reflect emotional ones that are being substituted for through the flesh. Whatever the case, fasting successfully—denying oneself food, or cigarettes, or coffee, or television—might free your mind to think more clearly and your body to exist healthier, while at least attempting to fast might help you discover who you are as a person by revealing to you what you are not able to do without. In the end, it will be your own human will which will determine your success at denying your flesh, a practice that is recommended here as a means of bringing your body under control and freeing it from an enslavement that inhibits further spiritual and practical growth.

39. Communicate More With Family

Family is important and a solid tradition in the black community. There was a time when we all had to stick together to survive. Not so much anymore. But the point here is that these people—these family members, both immediate and extended—these people know you. They are part of your history, your very essence. You share the same blood. One could even say that you share some of the same habits and thought patterns of your loved ones, some as distant as a second cousin or a great aunt or uncle, or even a grandmother or father. My father's mother and myself, for example, don't always eye to eye, but I love her and I know that she wants the best for me. Some of my best memories are of going to her house on the weekends where she would cook for me (she was a good cook) and dispense as much wisdom as she could in the three hours or so I would be there. Then we might play cards and watch a little television. Over the years, I came to see how similar she and I were in some habits. She is soft spoken, for the most part, and somewhat of a loner life myself. My other grandmother, meanwhile, the complete opposite of my father's mother, nevertheless also exhibits some qualities like my own. Like me, she can be loyal, pro-black, and a little pushy and impatient. The two women are different but I share qualities they both have and I am grateful. In fact, I am on speaking terms with nearly every member of my family that I know. I am an only child but I grew up with a large number of cousins, aunts and uncles and I love them all. Now I realize that I might be unique in this respect and that my family might be unique in this respect, but it's all in how you put yourself out and all in the value you place in your familial relationships. I place a high value on them.

My advice here is that if you are coming from a bad family situation, try to make it better. At least try and communicate. Just like fasting, and all the others listed above, try to do things piecemeal. For example, try to reach out to a particularly difficult family member through another member that you might be close with. If you do not feel that you are able to do it alone, use another for help. It might work out for you. Why do it in the first place? Because it is better in this life to be allied with and in loving relationships with as many people as possible. The love between two or three is much stronger than the solitude and loneliness of the individual. And it *should* be natural to be allied with family members.

Finally, I will relate an anecdote. Recently, I had to take a summer job just to make ends meet. On the job, I met an older woman who related to me that she had a son.

"Where's he now?" I asked the woman.

"Jail," she replied coldly.

"You ever see him?" I asked, really wanting to know and not just being nosy.

"No," she replied bitterly and flatly. When I asked why, she went on to illuminate things that her son had done when he was only 16 years old, things that she was still not willing to forgive or forget. At the time of our conversation, her son was in his 30s. Being my pushy self, trying to extract some love out of a seemingly dead relationship between the two of them, I suggested that she go and see her son in jail. But she balked violently, telling me that what I had suggested would not happen in a million years. Well, what happened, even to my own surprise about a month later, was that one morning she revealed to me that out of the blue her son had shown up at her home over the weekend. She was not happy about it and it was not clear if he had been in jail at all. I gathered that she had speculated he had been there based on his behavior and length of absence from her presence. Nevertheless, his visit was a shock to her, and one that she had to admit humbly to me. I didn't want to push it at this point, but I could notice a slight alteration in her tone of voice and character, as if she had been witness to some kind of miracle, as I don't believe that she had ever expected to see the boy again. I just smiled in the backseat of the car in which we were driving, happy that I might have succeeded in bringing two family members together. Always close to my own mother, I could not stand by and see such estrangement between another mother and son and my hope after leaving my co-worker behind not long after the revelation was that my advice might color all future interactions with her son in a positive way. And this is what I seek to do here: to add seasoning to bland familial relationships, to strengthen bonds year round, not just on holidays, to help understand that family members are human too and need love, and to encourage the life-long communication of family members with one another for mutual understanding and support.

38. Take Some Classes

This goes to my assertion that knowledge is power. This is true and taking classes has many benefits, gaining knowledge being one of them. But taking classes at universities and community colleges and in private organizations can have other benefits as well. It can introduce you to other people with other ideas, introducing you to new fellowship with other individuals with different ideas or unique perspectives on ideas you might already have. You might meet a friend or even a mate while taking a class. However, knowledge is the key and there are classes in today's world offering knowledge in all kinds of subjects, some of them often too silly to mention; but it is up to the individual what areas of study he or she might want to pursue. And you do not necessarily have to pursue a degree when you take a class. One might take an extended learning class in flower arrangement. This might seem silly and uninteresting to some but for the person interested in this class—which might take six weeks or so, meeting one night a week—the benefits from the knowledge gained might me very supportive in that individual's personal growth. No class taken would be too silly for that person sincerely interested in personal growth.

37. Dedicate Yourself To Your Child

Your child represents the future of your family and the future of the world. So why not treat that youngster as if he or she is a prince or a queen. This does not mean spoiling or coddling or letting them get away with whatever they want. In fact, discipline is important to your child's development. Teaching right and wrong early on can give the child a balanced and fair-minded way to see the world, and teach them to treat others the way they want to be treated. The other extremes are a spoiled child who is impatient and expects everything their way and is unwilling to work with and learn from others; and then there is the completely amoral child, who knows no shame, guilt, dignity or respect because he or she never learned this in the household.

I must stop here and preface first that I support two-parent, heterosexual households. Make of this what you will and apply any political connections to my viewpoint that you will. I cannot stop you from doing this. But going on from here, with my male-female, two parent model in mind, I realize that such a model does not exist to the extent that it did when I was growing up, due to divorce, children born out of wedlock and other evolving social values. This said, it is nevertheless important, even in the one parent home, for the parent to do his or her best to properly prepare the child every step of the way to deal with the world he or she may confront. The child, in my opinion, should be prepared to confront the world in which the adult parent currently exists. If the adult parent is a female, then other male role models, teachers, relatives, and church folk can substitute time with the youths from time to time. If the parent is a man, then appropriate women, aunts, mothers and grandmothers can help in the child rearing. There are always alternatives.

The point is that children are the clay and parents are the potters and the parents must take their roles in shaping their children's lives with the utmost seriousness. In fact, it should be a seriousness unto death. Parents should be willing to die for their children. Do not have them if you are not willing to make the ultimate sacrifices for their well-beings and their futures. Not to do so makes you a hypocrite and insensitive to the desires of others, especially children, who are the weakest and most vulnerable.

36. Attach Yourself To A Charity

A recurring theme in this list is the giving of the self, as I am a huge opponent of selfishness and vanity. I believe that to the detriment of this world, we are now in the middle of an age where pleasing the self has nearly become the chief end of existence. The problem will come when that individual wanting to please him or herself above the desires and concerns of all others arrives on the world scene, that individual of the highest order of vanity and self-concern. The author Tom Wolfe wrote about a New York City in his fiction as being a <u>Bonfire of the Vanities</u>. I speak of a nation now more vane than ever before in history, indeed a world on the verge of complete self-absorption. Under such a new, blatant and shamelessly self-serving regime, I submit that it would breath winds of fresh air into our souls if we were to give to some charitable causes, whether it be to churches, the homeless, or starving nations, not out of selfish desires to appear to be doing the right thing, but in attempts to discover where our hearts' concerns truly lie. What do we really feel? In fact, the perfect test in giving to a charity that our "hearts" lead us to would be to give to a charity but not let anyone else know of our donations. Keeping our charity a secret to ourselves might eliminate the potential swelling of pride that might come with public recognition. Then after we gave, we would be able to see, or our hearts would tell us, how satisfied we are with our acts. In other words, did we give for the right reasons or not?

However, we are encouraged to give to the needy and less fortunate—to cleave open our quickly closing hearts as Americans, as much as our wallets. But always we should give and be willing to do so for the "right" reasons.

35. Do Something To Better Race Relations

No man is an island. We all need one another to some degree. Human contact and interaction is essential to survival. Believe it or not white people need black people and black people need whites. Forget for a moment how slavery began and its history. I am talking about the here and now. Whites and blacks have grown up together in America—like brothers and sisters. And though over the years we have often existed as a dysfunctional family, two groups cannot grow up so close together and share so much, good and bad, and not establish a bond on some deeper level. It is my belief that the bond between the black and the white American will always run deeper than the ones involving any of the other races on the American landscape, Hispanic, Asian, or otherwise, because the black and the white in this country have too much history.

Here I will give another anecdote: When I was stuck on that Caribbean island years ago, I found myself down and out on an area called the Carenage, a lovely inlet that acted as a small port of call. As I sat there pondering some of the mistakes I had made in my life, two white tourists pulled up next to me. Immediately I recognized their accent as American. Americans at that time in the early 1990s did not travel to Grenada like Europeans did, so their accent stood out profoundly against the Caribbean patois I had become accustomed to. They stood there for a few moments trying to find their way before, I assume, thinking that I was a native, asked me an island-related question. When I responded with an intelligent, American sounding accent like their own, they were as surprised as I was and there was a light in their eyes, as there was in my own, as if I had discovered two long lost relatives on some desert outpost. At that moment, it did not matter that they (a husband and wife) were white and I was black. That all faded into the background and with them I had one of the purest—though brief—conversations with two white people I have ever had in my life. To really feel and understand what I mean, one would have to have been there. But you can take it from me. There is a relationship beneath the surface that "most" of us, black and white, are ashamed or afraid to admit exists. To throw off the shackles of slavery that continue to bind blacks and whites alike, neither of must be afraid to embrace this bond beneath the surface, based on growing up on American soil under the same sun.

But this collection of brief essays is addressed to black people in particular. Your responsibility in this matter is to acknowledge friction and discomfort with your white brothers and sisters when you see it occur and then to address it directly without fear or shame. This is the challenge for black people, to overcome the bitterness of the past and to reach out despite it. This is a heavy task, heavier for some than others. But it would have its rewards. The fact is that since Civil Rights laws are now solidly on the books, we must face racism at the individual level, among those people whom legislation has not affected the heart. And there are many of them out there. I am not so naïve as to deny this. What this makes us all, black people, are sometimes individual Civil Rights campaigns, where we have to fight one on one to get justice. There remain national bodies to defend us like the NAACP, but in many cases, some race-based decisions and interactions are quick, come quick and require quick responses and resolutions. In light of this, in light of our new positions as individual race warriors, I submit to black people a new tactic of relating beneath the surface with those white brothers and sisters, of finding those things that we share in common, as opposed to differences, to establish relationships, even friendships.

34. Increase Your Knowledge
Of History

Don't just get to know the history that concerns you yourself and those of your kind. Get to know that history of the world in general. Get to know those obscure facts that might round out your education. Get to know what it might have felt like when it was discovered that the world was round, or when it was discovered that the earth was the center of the solar system and occupied only a tiny portion of the vast universe. Get to know American history and then would history. First, I would recommend, getting to know those things that have been established as objective fact, such as discovering that the world is round, as such information is less easily biased by subjective interpretation. Bias leads to revision and misinterpretation of history and black people are often suspicious of the "white man's" writing of history. This is why it helps to research those objective things first before investigating the history of those supporting factors around important historical events. No one will know exactly what happened 300 or 400 years ago. No one will know the details, what the actors of those times were thinking while they were doing what they were doing. As time goes by, we can only estimate the reasons and specifics behind historic events. What we can do, however, in my opinion, is to extrapolate the meanings of those events, based on the events of modern history that is already a part of our memories because we have lived them. Human nature has not changed all that much, it is my opinion, since the beginning of time; therefore, we can speculate on much of history based on what we know and how we live today.

To begin research into human history, I would recommend first looking into areas that might interest you. Then I would find the most consistently referenced material on that area—the one bandied about and
discussed most—and read that material and see where you come down
on it. This will allow you to enter the debate, for example, on the history of slavery, the history of the United States, of Africa, or Europe,
the American space program, or what have you. This will allow you to
figure out where you might come down on a given subject. From there,
you might want to read less popular, more obscure, even critical material on the same subject matter to see what the not as well known are
saying; and by reading the popular and less popular side by side you
will have a well rounded perspective on your historical subject matter.

The point is to increase your knowledge of where you and your world
come from. This might enable you to discover your position more
clearly in the world in which we all now live.

33. Travel A Short Distance From Home

Get to know the immediate environment that you take for granted. Growing up in Washington, D.C. where I was born, I never once took the free tours of the White House or the Monument. I just took them for granted, while the tourists to Washington reveled in them. I did visit the Lincoln Memorial and the Air and Space museum on a number of occasions over the years, mostly because these attractions were open to the public, requiring no waiting. However, generally speaking, I took my beautiful city, and its lovely classical architecture and monuments for granted. Most people do this, I get the feeling, after having lived in the San Francisco Bay Area, where crossing the Golden Gate Bridge is a routine affair for many.

Upon a recent return to Washington, however, I made a point to pay a visit to the National Gallery of Art to see some of the great European masterpieces, as I am a fan of great art. I had never been there before to "really" look around.

Washington now is an international city—becoming so more and more every day—and there is a lot to see and a lot of history. But even if you live in a small community, there is much you can take advantage of in your immediate environment. Every place has its own unique history and some place where there is some kind of natural beauty to be beheld. Of, course I cannot speak for everyone, but it would not hurt to connect more with one's immediate surroundings to instill a sense of community and pride in one's community. Respect for one's community, no matter how dreary and squalid, might go a long way to appreciating what one has. Such appreciation might even lead to a spirit of wanting to make improvements.

So when I say take short trips away from home, I mean to take trips to discover what exists within a 50 to 60 mile radius of where you live. This will allow you to claim these places for yourself and your particular district. Discover a park, a field, a pond, a broken down playground, an adjoining community, a restaurant and appreciate what you see, understand them and consider making contributions or improvement if necessary.

32. Travel A Long Distance From Home

Ever been to Africa for a vacation? Neither have I. But I want to go one day. Some of it has to do with "exploring my roots," but just as much, if not more, has to do with wanting to spend time in a completely natural, exotic environment. This is an expensive proposition and going, depends on one's desire to make such a trip happen, while making such a trip happen will say much about you. The point in traveling a long distance from home is to lose yourself in another environment completely. Believe me, you can "find yourself" when you travel far away from where you are and immerse yourself in another culture and among people not like yourself. (Hopefully, those people will be friendly to you).

But even negative long distance travel experiences can be beneficial in their educational value. My advice for long distance trips from home would be to first travel somewhere you have always wanted go and see if it fits into what you expected of it. If it does, go again, but don't restrict yourself to that location always. Visit another place and compare it to the one before. Over time, become more daring. If you find yourself a Caribbean fan, like myself, try another tropical or beach environment like South America, Hawaii or the Mediterranean to compare. Always, of course, do your homework and brush up on safety matters before you set out, as we Americans can't always travel everywhere. But you are encouraged here to jump out of your safe environment and explore, if you are so able. Traveling is another means of opening and expanding the mind.

31. Save Money

No, it's not easy to save money. Frankly, I don't even know what "save" means when it comes to money, when money is realistically just a bargaining tool to get what we want. Toward that end, money has to eventually be used to get what we want and what we need. I guess then, instead of "saving" money, we should learn to exercise some controls over our needs and wants.

Sure, it is helpful to be thrifty when it comes to money, to keep some in store for difficult times or to save for the future. But perhaps it would help more to tame our desires. We should evaluate or reevaluate exactly what our needs are. Do we have to have this or that garment; do you have to eat out more than twice a week? Must we have that particular car at all costs? These are basic questions dealing with wants and needs and this is what life comes down to, taking care of wants and needs. But needs come first and they are basic: food, water, shelter, clothing. Beyond these come the evaluations of what else we consider important to our daily lives. It is obvious that some of us cannot help but to live in "high style." However, do not be deceived by advertising which tells you that you need things that you don't have or have never before wanted. You must be honest with yourself and if you are, then the money saving stands a chance of falling right into place. If you desire little, no matter how much you might make at your work, then you will spend little.

Black people in particular have a history of wanting the biggest and best. This does have to be. Exercise some material control once in a while. This might even lead to be unique kind of peace of mind.

30. Write Letters Instead Of Using E-mail

Difficult. I know. In this high tech, overly accelerated world we live in. But what are we speeding up to and why are we going so fast? What's the hurry? These are questions we need to ask ourselves. The idea of writing letters is to slow things down, to get a bead on one's thoughts and feelings. There is also an artistic element to handwriting. I learned this is school. Each of us has a signature unique to us and, therefore, writing styles that are unique. In writing letters by hand—once and a while—we might explore those styles, in addition of course, to surprising and pleasing those receiving our letters. Writing also allows us to explore our thoughts as the words come from our pens and while in exploring our thoughts we enter unique worlds that bring on us a kind of calm. One never knows—in writing by hand, you might discover that there is a writer inside you waiting to get out. In fact, I have always considered black people—including myself—to be very expressive and literary minded people, but many of us do not explore this side of ourselves. Just as we have always been good storytellers and entertainers, I believe there is a vast and untapped literary mind out there dormant in the black community. There always has been. Let's take advantage of it, now that we have access to so much to facilitate our development as writers.

Many are now taking advantage, I must say. Black writers of novels and self-help guides flower in abundance and they are good examples of what I am talking about. These people like Omar Tyree, Terry McMillan and, of course, Toni Morrison and Alice Walker and others had something to say, and they said it, sometimes profoundly.

But start out writing by hand, perhaps in a journal, to get a feel for what you want to say on a deep level. Writing by hand, if nothing else, makes you more patient because you have to bring your thoughts under control in order to conform to the speed of the writing mode, as opposed to typing, where some people are able to type almost as fast as they think. Start with a letter to a friend or a close relative and see how it goes. "Dear Mom…" for example, or "My Dearest Wife…"

29. Write a Letter To Your Representative

Within all our communities, there is something that we are unhappy with, whether major or minor. While I do not advocate picking a fight with the government here, I would encourage you to write a letter to your congressman addressing a specific matter in your community. If there are no dramatic problems, then don't bother. But if there are, and you think your representative can or should do something about it, then let him or her know, whether you voted for them or not, whether they are member of your party or not. The fact is that they hold the position and are obligated to serving "all" the people, all the time.

With this letter, however, you are encouraged to be as professional as possible; therefore, writing by hand is not encouraged and e-mail, in fact, might prove more effective, in getting through to the right person. But you never know, it might help instead, to sit down at a typewriter or computer, bang out a letter addressed to your representative and then put it into an envelope. People do still read mail after all, while e-mail can easily be read and discarded, sorry to say, with the press of a button. So called "snail mail" still has some value in its physical substance and the appreciation of the effort put into it.

A second reason for addressing a congressman, or senator from one's state, (whomever you feel would get the job done) is to get you more directly involved in the political process and again, through writing, to discover how you feel about the issue you choose to address. It is easy to call into a radio, TV program or talk show and vent one's displeasure, but such activity can be primitive and seem sometimes almost like road rage. Writing a letter is more professional and classier and gives you a chance, as I said, to think about what you feel and what you want to say. After this, if you get no response, then there is nothing wrong with a follow up call to see if your letter was received or addressed. Lastly, I would say, in the professionalism of your letter, make it as long as possible, with as many details as possible, to let the reader know that you are up on the issue and that you are serious about its solution. Lengthy, in depth letters put their readers on the hot seat. Quick jabs are just like calling into a talk show, and the readers of such letters know this—that you are just venting. And again, the longer the letter, the more you get into the issue and how you feel about it.

28. Walk The Halls Of Your Old High School

High school was a critical period in our lives. Some people might over-estimate its important, as if it formed who we are today. While I do not go this far, the importance of high school experience also cannot be underestimated, whether our schools were "good or bad." High school represented the transition period between child and adulthood. There is no doubt about this. We were formed and shaped in high school in ways that we might not even be able to put into words. I don't know about anyone else, but high school for me was a blur. I cannot to this day remember that many specific events; but I do remember specific faces and their personalities. My point here is that it might help to recover ourselves by reminiscing. Walking the grounds of one's old school can give that warm and fuzzy feeling that may be absent from your life today. There is no corniness here. Reliving old memories, times and experiences can enable to us to "feel" again, and we all need to "feel" again, as this world we live in seems to get colder, more tech-nological and mechanical each and every day. Machines do not have emotions. We do. Sometimes we need to rediscover them, or discover them for the first time. Walking the grounds of one's old haunts can help one recover some valuable lost feelings.

27. Walk the Grounds Of Your Old College Or University

For those of you who attended college, walking the grounds of your old school could revive one's spirit as well. The benefits of this experience would be that the memories of college would probably be more vivid, as what happened was not as far back as high school and you were older in college and perhaps better equipped to remember. (Though, this is not necessarily the case for sure. For many, college was as much a blur as high school). But college, for those who went, was a unique experience.

When I went back to the University of Virginia for the first time, I attended a football game. It was nothing like when I went when we were freshman. There was a lot more energy and excitement as an undergraduate while I felt much more matured walking the grounds years later. I felt like an adult and I felt a sense of accomplishment having "conquered" the rigors of UVA to attain a degree in English literature. I believe that most people have this experience when they return: a feeling of accomplishment. Also, they would have pride in their schools as alma maters and memories of fun times, as there is always partying going on at all colleges. Therefore, the college and high school experience memories would probably be different, though neither could triumph over the other, depending on the person doing the recollecting.

In the end, I would advise returning to one's college setting to soak in the sense of accomplishment so that you can appreciate more what you have after looking back with pride in what you had to overcome to get there. As black people in particular, we should be happy, grateful, and thankful for our opportunities and accomplishments. It was not all that long ago that we were not allowed to attend college at all.

26. Read Some Black Literature

Generally speaking, black people should support other black people. There's nothing wrong with this. It used to be that way naturally, and blacks appreciate support from other blacks. Other ethnic groups support one another. Why shouldn't we, and reading each other's work is just one example, and reading is just one example, as we can sample works of art of those like us, and patronize the businesses of our own in all areas. There is much among black culture to be scrutinized. I target literature here because again, this specific form of art, to me, exposes the soul of the writer. The writer, all writers, are trying to communicate something deep to you, something deeply important to them, something, in almost all cases, that the black writer wants to communicate to all black people everywhere, throughout time. These people need to be read. Indeed, most black writers scream to have their works read. But what should we read?

I recommend reading the works of some of the great black writers, the ones who wrote early in the past century, the works of Richard Wright, James Baldwin and Ralph Ellison, in addition to WEB Dubois, Booker T. Washington and Frederick Douglas. Read the works of the writers who set the stage for today, the writers who wrote before Civil Rights and integration. Reading these writers of slave times and Jim Crow will give us an idea of the pressures under which they wrote and the times in which they lived. This might give us a greater appreciation of what we have today.

After reading these earlier writers, I would then settle on some later writers like those of the Harlem Renaissance such as Langston Hughes and Zora Neale Hurston, before moving to modern times and the works of Toni Morrison and Henry Louis Gates to name a few. In other words, read the works of the great black writers from the beginning until now to get a sense of how times have changed and the thinking of writers have changed over time. This will give you, the reader, a chance to see where we as blacks have come as a people through the things we have written about and show us where we might be headed. I guarantee you the results of this "reading" investigation will be fascinating. Especially if you start your reading with the earliest slave writings and then make your way through history. And do not restrict yourself to fiction, but non-fiction as well. The non-fiction writers like Dubois are among the earliest radical, pro-Black and philosophical writers.

25. View Some Classic Black Cinema

Particularly in the 1970s, there has been some strong work done in black cinema. Black people made and starred in some good, nearly great, films in that decade. Black presence in film dates back way before then, to perhaps, the 1940s, but the fruit of our liberation on film, due to the Civil Rights movement in the 1960s, truly blossomed in the 1970s. I think of films that are somewhat hard to come by today like "Buck and the Preacher," "Claudine," "Come Back Charleston Blue," and "The Liberation of L.B. Jones" when I think of the black-made and acted films from the 1970s that had me, a young boy growing up then, riveted to the screen. In the 1980s, blacks became known for comedies and making people laugh on film. But the 1970s was a water-shed decade, where there was complete artistic freedom and integrity. The films mentioned above reflect only a sampling of some of the genius that existed in that decade and that needs to be preserved. They need to be preserved by people like us. My advice for anyone wanting to investigate the treasure of films made in the 70s would be to do an Internet search and then come up with a list of films made during that decade. Many of those films have come to be known as "blaxploita-tion," meaning that blacks are on some levels made fun of and stereo-typed in some films as thugs, prostitutes and pimps. While there are many of these, like "Coffee," "Foxy Brown" and "Superfly," there were also many excellent works that came from that decade.

Just like the reading of more black literature, it might behoove we black people to take a tour of black presence in film beginning from our first presence on the big screen until now. It would be up to us to identify the high and low points of our presence there. It would also be up to us not to take for granted our presence on the big screen and to examine carefully the substance of the things we had to say when we are up there. When we appear in a movie what does it mean to us as a people? What has been, or is being said, that affects us all, and in what ways, in all black movies?

A last word of advice would be to first view the "serious" movies of the 1970s and then to view the comedies and those of other genres. This would be if you were to start with black film in the 1970s in your examination. But you might also want to start from the beginning, before and after World War II. However, if you do start in the 70s, start with the serious movies. These movies like "Claudine" and others speak to the depth of a black experience that cannot be ignored, then or now.

24. Review Some Statistics Of Modern African-American Life

The numbers are not hopeful or impressive, and we have all heard them before: in school, on the news, in textbooks, at the barbershop and other places. Probably the most hopeful number when it comes to African American demographics is the steady population percentage that blacks have always maintained in these United States over the years. Unlike the Indians, blacks have survived "the American Experiment," for the most part. We were not "wiped out." For perhaps 100 years, we have maintained that solid area of between 12 and 20 percent of the general American population. And our numbers do not show any signs of waning despite our problems, which are many.

What is changing, however, is that we are no longer the second largest minority in the United States. The Hispanics are, while other minorities, Asians and Europeans, are also on the rise in numbers and sociopolitical influence. Now we all live in an age now where we are all urged to get along with one another and to respect each other's differences and uniqueness. This is fine, but there will always be those things essentially black that I believe will always be worth protecting and must be protected. These areas, which involve our unique history and character as a people, should never be lost, forgotten or sacrificed for some nebulous, New Agey idea of some collective "greater good," imposed by man on other men. The black American like the Jew is a unique individual, with a unique voice, unique past and a unique wisdom. Never forget that. We have brought peace to America through our struggles and have inspired the world at large through our endurance, struggles, love and compassion for our fellow men. I am proud to be a

Black American. In an ironic twist, it is my personal belief that America might have never endured in the first place had we not been brought over here. But this point is for another discussion entirely.

Now the bad news: Since we were removed from Africa and brought to America, we have been up against it. We have suffered as a people in this nation from day one and it continues. Regarding the modern day statistical numbers that I encourage you to peruse at length to understand that fellow blacks continue to suffer, they involve following: black men are still in jail in inordinate numbers. This fact is mind-boggling. Roughly only six percent of the population, but nearly 50 percent in jail. Sure, many are committing the crimes, but they operate in a system designed against them and a history not kind to them; most serious disease rates are highest among blacks; drugs and alcohol still plague our communities as does mental illness, all again, in inordinate numbers. Add to these stats, those concerning AIDS contraction and mortality rates, suicide rates and general health disparities such as heart disease and hypertension and you have a despairing picture of the future of black America. But then again we have been there before.

The statistics, which we should all read from time to time, and which are not pretty, bear it all up. Some of us might want to ignore the statistics. But we cannot. This would amount to a monstrous form of denial. We are still suffering as a people! We have made great strides for sure, but the overwhelming majority of us have been left behind and live in squalor. I don't want to guilt trip anyone. I only encourage the reading of the statistics on the conditions of your own people to see where your own heart leads you. It might lead you to turn the other cheek, or it might encourage you to get involved and help your brothers and sisters to not just preserve and perpetuate our ethnic group but to help it grow and even blossom. This should be the goal.

23. Read Martin Luther King Jr's "I Have a Dream Speech" Over Again

The historic speech, delivered on the steps at the Lincoln Memorial in Washington D.C. on August 28, 1963, is repeated here in its entirety. You are encouraged to read it. It is a piece of living history. And take your time.

Five score years ago, a great American, in whose symbolic shadow we stand signed the Emancipation Proclamation. This momentous decree came as a great beacon light of hope to millions of Negro slaves who had been seared in the flames of withering injustice. It came as a joyous daybreak to end the long night of captivity. But one hundred years later, we must face the tragic fact that the Negro is still not free.

One hundred years later, the life of the Negro is still sadly crippled by the manacles of segregation and the chains of discrimination. One hundred years later, the Negro lives on a lonely island of poverty in the midst of a vast ocean of material prosperity. One hundred years later, the Negro is still languishing in the corners of American society and finds himself an exile in his own land.

So we have come here today to dramatize an appalling condition. In a sense we have come to our nation's capital to cash a check. When the architects of our republic wrote the magnificent words of the Constitution and the Declaration of Independence, they were signing a promissory note to which every American was to fall heir.

This note was a promise that all men would be guaranteed the inalienable rights of life, liberty, and the pursuit of happiness. It is obvious today that America has defaulted on this promissory note insofar as her citizens of color are concerned. Instead of honoring this sacred obligation, America has given the Negro people a bad check which has come back marked "insufficient funds." But we refuse to believe that the bank of justice is bankrupt. We refuse to believe that there are insufficient funds in the great vaults of opportunity of this nation.

So we have come to cash this check—a check that will give us upon demand the riches of freedom and the security of justice. We have also come to this hallowed spot to remind America of the fierce urgency of now. This is no time to engage in the luxury of cooling off or to take the tranquilizing drug of gradualism. Now is the time to rise from the dark and desolate valley of segregation to the sunlit path of racial justice. Now is the time to open the doors of opportunity to all of God's children. Now is the time to lift our nation from the quicksands of racial injustice to the solid rock of brotherhood.

It would be fatal for the nation to overlook the urgency of the moment and to underestimate the determination of the Negro. This sweltering summer of the Negro's legitimate discontent will not pass until there is an invigorating autumn of freedom and equality. Nineteen sixty-three is not an end, but a beginning. Those who hope that the Negro needed to blow off steam and will now be content will have a rude awakening if the nation returns to business as usual. There will be neither rest nor tranquility in America until the Negro is granted his citizenship rights.

The whirlwinds of revolt will continue to shake the foundations of our nation until the bright day of justice emerges. But there is something that I must say to my people who stand on the warm threshold which leads into the palace of justice. In the process of gaining our rightful place we must not be guilty of wrongful deeds. Let us not seek to satisfy our thirst for freedom by drinking from the cup of bitterness and hatred.

We must forever conduct our struggle on the high plane of dignity and discipline. We must not allow our creative protest to degenerate into physical violence. Again and again we must rise to the majestic heights of meeting physical force with soul force.

The marvelous new militancy which has engulfed the Negro community must not lead us to distrust of all white people, for many of our white brothers, as evidenced by their presence here today, have come to realize that their destiny is tied up with our destiny and their freedom is inextricably bound to our freedom.

We cannot walk alone. And as we walk, we must make the pledge that we shall march ahead. We cannot turn back. There are those who are asking the devotees of civil rights, "When will you be satisfied?" we can never be satisfied as long as our bodies, heavy with the fatigue of travel, cannot gain lodging in the motels of the highways and the hotels of the cities. We cannot be satisfied as long as the Negro's basic mobility is from a smaller ghetto to a larger one. We can never be satisfied as long as a Negro in Mississippi cannot vote and a Negro in New York believes he has nothing for which to vote. No, no, we are not satisfied, and we will not be satisfied until justice rolls down like waters and righteousness like a mighty stream.

I am not unmindful that some of you have come here out of great trials and tribulations. Some of you have come fresh from narrow cells. Some of you have come from areas where your quest for freedom left you battered by the storms of persecution and staggered by the winds of police brutality. You have been the veterans of creative suffering. Continue to work with the faith that unearned suffering is redemptive.

Go back to Mississippi, go back to Alabama, go back to Georgia, go back to Louisiana, go back to the slums and ghettos of our northern cities, knowing that somehow this situation can and will be changed. Let us not wallow in the valley of despair. I say to you today, my friends, that in spite of the difficulties and frustrations of the moment, I still have a dream. It is a dream deeply rooted in the American dream.

I have a dream that one day this nation will rise up and live out the true meaning of its creed: "We hold these truths to be self-evident: that all men are created equal." I have a dream that one day on the red hills of Georgia the sons of former slaves and the sons of former slaveowners will be able to sit down together at a table of brotherhood. I have a dream that one day even the state of Mississippi, a desert state, sweltering with the heat of injustice and oppression, will be transformed into an oasis of freedom and justice. I have a dream that my four children will one day live in a nation where they will not be judged by the color of their skin but by the content of their character. I have a dream today.

I have a dream that one day the state of Alabama, whose governor's lips are presently dripping with the words of interposition and nullification, will be transformed into a situation where little black boys and black girls will be able to join hands with little white boys and white girls and walk together as sisters and brothers. I have a dream today. I have a dream that one day every valley shall be exalted, every hill and mountain shall be made low, the rough places will be made plain, and the crooked places will be made straight, and the glory of the Lord shall be revealed, and all flesh shall see it together. This is our hope. This is the faith with which I return to the South. With this faith we will be able to hew out of the mountain of despair a stone of hope. With this faith we will be able to transform the jangling discords of our nation into a beautiful symphony of brotherhood. With this faith we will be able to work together, to pray together, to struggle together, to go to jail together, to stand up for freedom together, knowing that we will be free one day.

This will be the day when all of God's children will be able to sing with a new meaning, "My country, 'tis of thee, sweet land of liberty, of thee I sing. Land where my fathers died, land of the pilgrim's pride, from every mountainside, let freedom ring." And if America is to be a great nation, this must become true. So let freedom ring from the prodigious hilltops of New Hampshire. Let freedom ring from the mighty mountains of New York. Let freedom ring from the heightening Alleghenies of Pennsylvania! Let free-

dom ring from the snowcapped Rockies of Colorado! Let freedom ring from the curvaceous peaks of California! But not only that; let freedom ring from Stone Mountain of Georgia! Let freedom ring from Lookout Mountain of Tennessee! Let freedom ring from every hill and every molehill of Mississippi. From every mountainside, let freedom ring.

When we let freedom ring, when we let it ring from every village and every hamlet, from every state and every city, we will be able to speed up that day when all of God's children, black men and white men, Jews and Gentiles, Protestants and Catholics, will be able to join hands and sing in the words of the old Negro spiritual, "Free at last! free at last! thank God Almighty, we are free at last!"

Wow!!! Dr. King was a man full of hope. What stands out for me is that our promise as a people remains unfulfilled, that we can be even greater and accomplish even greater things than we have already have. Dr. King also had hope for America. He believed deeply in America. For me, the most striking passage signaling complete and unfettered equality among the races comes with the following: "No, no, we are not satisfied, and we will not be satisfied until justice rolls down like waters and righteousness like a mighty stream." This image is powerful, overwhelming and unmistakable in its implications. It is a natural image where nature moves of its own power and nothing stands in its path. What Dr. King meant I think in this passage is that nature is not a thinking entity. It moves without rationality and for Dr. King, he would have an America based in justice and freedom for all men and women to the point where believing in justice and freedom principles would be as natural a thing as breathing, the beating of the heart or the blowing of the wind. This America would occupy a spiritual realm.

Sadly to say, however, that this America does not exist today. But it can exist one day and this is the United States that Dr. King saw in his vision. We have come a long way, but we are still not there and all, whites, blacks and other races, have to work together to make it happen. For blacks, it important to reflect on Dr. King's words to give us an idea of where we have come from and on the hope that still exists for ourselves and America in the future. We must remember the hope and remember that we are not there yet. We'll know when we are there, just as we all have intuitive knowledge of what it will take to get there.

22. Review The History Of Slavery And The Civil War

As painful and potentially painstaking as this might be, reviewing this history will help you put past, present and future in perspective. Going into the new century, let us not forget the past of the past century—or the past in general—lest we repeat them. Something as vile as slavery will never return to the United States but it might provide we blacks with some valuable insight into human nature to know how American slavery started, why it started, what happened while it was going on, why and how it finally ended. I for one have always been curious. When, for example, did the first impulse to enslave the black man enter the white man? Did this impulse enter one man who then infected many others? Was it a mob mentality? What happened when the eyes of the black man met the eyes of the white for the first time? Was there any hope of peace in those initial interactions? Is the white man a naturally brutal creature, or is such brutality characteristic to all men? An investigation of history and the history of American slavery might shed some light here.

American slavery goes way, way back to the 1600s. But the Americans did not initiate it on a worldwide scale. The Spanish launched the sale and trade of African blacks among the white races. The British later joined in. Then the Americans. I find some of the details of slavery interesting, though always appalling.

As blacks, most of us are aware of the horrors of slavery, the beatings, whippings, the maiming, the rapes, the humiliations, the broken families, the lost dignity, the backbreaking work. But what about the mentality of the slave owner, his wife and children and neighbors? What kinds of people were these? Were they "evil" in say, a biblical sense? Knowledge of the characters of slave holders and their kind might shed even more light on how we see the world we live in now. What about the laws that were passed during slave times and those that the slaves were forced to submit to? What kinds of minds were capable of putting such laws that kept the slaves down into the books? What was the mentality back then? An investigation of that time might illuminate some thought processes. What made Lincoln make the decisions that he made? What kind of man was he? In a biblical sense, was Lincoln, a "good" man? On this score, I personally believe that Lincoln was a "good" man. But why did America go to war with itself? Was it for the slaves? Did our existence really force an entire country to go to war and almost destroy itself? Was the situation that dire? The little questions are the ones that can illuminate the big the picture most through their answers.

And again, a staunch review of our past can put our very lives in fresh perspective. The Jews do it several times each and every year, most notably with Passover, where they remember their deliverance by God, through Moses, from enslavement to the Egyptians. Was our situation really that much different and do we not owe a debt of gratitude to the memory of that deliverance, to the people who suffered and died for our freedoms today, to Lincoln, the man who signed the freedom orders and, like the Jews, to our God?

Black Americans are a chosen people as well, I believe. We have been brought to America for a reason, which may or not have been completely revealed to us as a people yet. We have never really reached a complete, collective consciousness of the reality and importance of our existences on this American soil; such a collective realization of this fact might amount to a new liberation of our souls. The first emancipation of blacks was physical (we were released from our chains); the second emancipation of the American black was legal (we were given the right to vote and—at least on paper—to live in equal partnership with our former slaveholders); the third emancipation was intellectual (we learned to accept ourselves as free, conscious and independent beings during the Black Power consciousness movements of the 1960s); but for American blacks, it is my opinion that the fourth, and hopefully final stage of our liberation, must be spiritual, where the American black must return to his God, make peace with his God, and put his fate into the hands of his God, where it really always has been.

21. Get To Know Your Children's Friends

For three reasons getting to know your children's friends would be helpful. One, this will give you insight into the mind of the next generation and with such insight, you might be able to provide some help and comfort to their minds. And your own kids won't mind. They would, in fact, after some curiosity, invite your interest into the activities of them and their friends—as long as you are not too intrusive. Secondly, you might get an idea into how your own child thinks by getting to know his or her friends on a first name, one to one basis. Your own child may be up to something detrimental to their well being and keeping in contact with a friend might serve to disrupt potential danger. And again, you are not "spying." You are getting to know your kid and his or her friends out of general concern, interest and friendship. And thirdly, as stated above, you might be able to provide some wisdom to the next generation. Believe it or not, parents possess wisdom they do not even realize. Some wisdom can be very simple, coming from life experiences. You need not have suffered much in life. All you have to have done is lived a certain number of years and you already possess knowledge and wisdom that your kids and their friends don't understand and don't know about. You are, therefore, a perfect person to lead them down paths that you know will serve them well. Your job is to steer them from paths that may have failed you or you have witnessed to fail others. The only obstacle is to develop the will to do so, to take out the time and effort and have the patience to talk to your kids and their friends. And this can be fun because kids have a lot of energy and say things that are often interesting. Many of their observations, in fact, possess the seeds of some later "wisdom" and their thoughts need to be guided in the best possible directions for success.

What can make such an investment in your kids' world worthwhile and fun would be close examinations and comparisons of how much your kids and their friends are like or unlike you and your friends were when you were coming up. There may be no similarities at all, but this itself can be of interest, a challenge, even a potentially rewarding challenge to find common ground. Your kids and their friends will appreciate your efforts if you are friendly, sincere and persistent in approaching them. The key is to always remember that you are putting "their" needs before your own. Realizing this seems to be a particular problem for many American parents these days.

20. Befriend Neighborhood Kids

Try to be a good neighbor—even if you live in a ghetto. Dependable people, people who go that extra step to say hello, be friendly and extend a helping hand to their fellow man, get respect and sometimes even extra protection, even in public housing, ghettoized complexes in America. I know this for a fact. Part of my extended family spent significant years in such an environment and I often visited such a complex when I was child in Washington, D.C. But my family had respect and love from their neighbors, even in their drug-riddled, often violent environment of concrete, mortar and brick. I do not ever remember seeing many trees in the complex.

But it is easy to let life experiences allow to you develop a hardened heart and to cut yourself off from those around you. This is a mistake, because in cutting yourself off you don't allow yourself and that unique "wisdom" that you possess to be shared with others, particularly the younger generation who need it the most. My point here regards the youth out there who need the help of us older folk most. We need to get out there, out of homes and from behind our closed curtains, and let the kids that are not our own know that they are loved and respected. As a neighbor, we need to give kind words to these kids when we pass by instead of walking by coldly. Negative behavior from strangers only engenders confusion and eventually coldness and bitterness among today's youth.

Yes it is true that many of the children out there are so-called "bad" kids, sometimes even mean and dangerous. This is true. Why is this true? Because no one ever showed them the respect and dignity over the years and such lack of attention and consideration has grown into mounds of discontent, sometimes manifesting itself in violence. As youths ourselves, if we take a moment to look back, we didn't want anyone ignoring, mistreating and disrespecting us. Why do we do it to today's kids, who are in many ways defenseless because they have not learned what we have? It is a vicious cycle. We grow into such behaviors and transfer these behaviors right back to the young. But the behaviors can be broken, with the proper attitudes toward youth and we can begin with the kids we see everyday right in our own neighborhoods. Once we get to know the kids in our own neighborhoods, we can work on the kids at large, those on buses and elsewhere and out in the streets.

The key is that once you get to know a solid sampling of the youth mind, you might be able to then relate to youths in general, males and females. Trust me adults, the youths need your help.

There are three obstacles out there, to getting to know kids, that speak volumes to our modern times, but which can be overcome. They are the fear of being labeled a sexual deviate for getting too close to kids, our natural aversions to penetrating youth minds, and our general fears and mistrust of modern youth. Firstly, yes, we must be careful of the degrees to which we extend kindness and helping hands to young people who are strangers. We live in a very paranoid world where even genuine "good" intentions can be misconstrued or misinterpreted. My advice for engaging a strange child is to do so first from a position of authority, through something like a stern hello. Let the child or youth know that you are a "serious" person, a person they might be able to learn something from, and a person who is not a threat to them either physically or emotionally. After a few such stern-faced, confident interactions with a youth, that youth might gain your trust as someone with confidence and leadership ability that they might be able to turn to for advice and friendship. Your hook in your sternness is that you will appear to be a person grounded in some truth or confidence they have never experienced.

Secondly, many adults do not want to deal with youth because they are intimidated. Kids, in their innocence, have a way of looking into the soul of adults like no others. Sorry. But this is a fact. And adults know it to be. Kids can look at an adult and see things in that adult that can make him or her uncomfortable and in many cases, kids are correct in the evaluations. What kids are good at is seeing flaws and exploiting them. Kids have natural gifts for this. But we must not me intimidated by the unique scrutiny of youths because at the end of the day, they are still kids and we should not take ourselves so seriously as adults as to let the gaze and banter of youth intimidate us. If they are right about our flaws and call us on them, so what? We should be bigger than our flaws as adults and should be willing to laugh at our own selves. We should be able to laugh at our own selves right along with the kids. As a defense, we can make it a game and expose their flaws too.

Thirdly, many of us are also intimidated by today's youth because of their newfound aggressive natures. Some kids today make us fear for our very lives and we do not want to deal with them for this very reason. I acknowledge this dilemma here and it is a very tragic one, one of the worst examples of the failings of modern times: that kids are now emboldened to kill like no other time in history. Well, my advice would still be to reach out. All of us have to take chances if we want to make differences in the lives of others, in our own and in the community at large. If we really see that things are bad and getting worse and we want to help, then we have to be willing to make sacrifices emotionally and intellectually. It is a matter of having the will to do so. Strong wills and good intentions can overcome fear and produce positive results, it is my contention here.

19. Volunteer Your Time Somewhere Challenging

Test yourself. See how tough you are once in a while. Instead of a physical or mental workout, conduct an emotional one for a change. Picture yourself for a moment at some urban recreation center with poor black kids who are clamoring loudly for attention, who have foul mouths, who are dressed poorly, and who don't want to pay attention and even fight amongst themselves from to time. Now imagine yourself in the middle of this emotional storm trying to make a difference as some kind of counselor, coach or instructor. Think you could handle it? If so, for how long? How soon before you think that you might crack up and run for cover? Or do you think that you could go the distance? You might never know until you try and I guarantee you that the need for such help is out there right now in every corner of this country, somewhere in every community. There are people out there dying for wisdom and leadership like yours, in addition to your commitment, energy and intelligence. Do you have it to give? Again, I do not mean to guilt trip. This is not my goal. I seek only to inspire you to consider—to consider the need, to consider your value, your skills, and your potential benefit to the world.

The fact is that our benefits to the world are great. Whether we are Ph. Ds and CEOs, nurses or poor laborers, we can all make a difference. Again, what makes the difference in whether we will reach out to help or not rests on our wills to do so. The general benefits of challenging ourselves is that we might be able to grow personally, to strengthen ourselves, or at the least, to discover where we might need to gain strength; the overall benefits of working with those of our kind in some challenging way is that we can help "them" grow, in addition to helping ourselves. Such cooperation can perpetuate the spirit of the species—the American black—and might even engender the sense of communal unity lost with "integration." Even while integrated amongst the nation at large, we can still be unified and stronger as a group amongst ourselves.

18. Take On A Physical Challenge

Remember I said that we must stay in shape? Well, the next goal in getting there would be undertaking a great task aimed at achieving maximum fitness. Like we pushed ourselves to the wall in an emotional way, we need to do so physically or at least try to do so. The first physical obstacle that comes to mind is training for and then running a complete marathon. This would do the trick. It would provide focus in terms of training and eating habits and the body would lose weight and gain fitness during the training process alone, not to mention the actual race. In the actual race, I would estimate the loss of some two to three thousand calories, not to mention the psychological benefits of having conquered such a distance. However, if training for and running a marathon is not your thing, pick a sport or activity that you might want to master and try to do so, whether it be tennis, volleyball, racquetball or basketball. For me, I have often noticed that I burn the most calories when I am engaged in some sort involving direct competition, in a situation where I must fight to win. The intensity of the contest makes me want to play harder and working harder I correspondingly burn more calories.

Also we must not shirk physical challenges. If someone asks you to help them to move from one place to another, for example, see this as an opportunity for a workout. The lifting will excite some otherwise dormant muscles. I suggest extreme forms of physical challenges because some people need that one specific, overriding goal to get them motivated, as opposed to spending time picking and choosing different diets, weight loss programs and exercise routines. Instead, pick one thing and focus on it to get you over the hump. And it helps to engage in something physical that you think you might enjoy.

17. Take On A Mental Challenge

You have been out of college for some 20 years now. How about taking the SATs again to see how you do? Maybe you can do better than you did the first time. Wouldn't it be interesting to find out? The idea here is to exercise the brain. Perhaps you have grown over the years to the point that your SAT score might jump 100 points. Push yourself and see.

Or how about reading <u>Moby-Dick</u>, one of the longest and most densely plotted and written novels in American history? Without the aid of criticism or Cliff Notes, try to get through the novel from cover to cover, discover what its all about, and then compare what you think to what has been written about it over the years. Or maybe one of Shakespeare's plays? All of these are difficult to various degrees.

Investigate some natural occurrence and see why and how it occurs, such as raining. We all take it for granted, but what makes it rain in nature, or snow for that matter? What makes the trees grow? What are stars comprised of? What makes the human heart beat? How does the brain operate? How am I able to think so clearly or so quickly or so slowly, for that matter? All of these questions and their answers make us think and exercise those brains of ours. The brain has to be worked out and you can become smarter. You can continue to gain knowledge if you have the will to do so. And you don't necessarily have to go back to school to learn. Just grab a textbook about some subject and investigate it on your own.

16. Meet A Black College Professor

They're out there. There are many of them. Most of them, men and women, probably teach at historically black colleges. But there are plenty at the more "traditional" colleges as well, including the elite Ivy League. There are some bright, gifted and highly educated black people out there, sharing their knowledge with others of all races. The problem is that the media does not usually give us a chance to see these men and women at their very best. Therefore we might have to go to them personally.

Some of them we do know well, like Henry Louis Gates, who is the Dean of Harvard University's Black Studies program and Dr. Cornel West, who occupies a similar position at Princeton University. These two black men are among America's most prominent university-affiliated scholars. But as I said, there are others out there. What we should do, to support their efforts and to learn from them, is to go meet them where they are if possible. They all have office hours at their schools. Professors are busy wherever they are, but if approached correctly they might be willing to talk and even offer some of their general opinions and knowledge. These academics need love and attention too. They need to know that they are not laboring in vain, that all their education has not amounted for naught. Particularly if you have kids, meeting a black university professor might fall right into your plans. You might even want to take your college bound child to meet a person who teaches in the field that your child aspires to. However, in the end, I encourage the support of the Black American academia for their own accomplishments. Because if you think about it, 200 years ago we, as a people, could not even read. We weren't even allowed to. Since that time, we have fought our ways into the most hallowed universities and have now reached the pinnacle of academic success. This success should not be taken for granted. Our scholars should be recognized and given our support.

15. Meet A Black Journalist Or Writer

I suggest this as journalists have much influence when it comes to popular public opinion and cultural influence. They have power. But we knew this already, as we see their work everyday. Black journalists out there, however, like black professors often toil in obscurity. They are out there working hard, many to make a difference for their own people, but no one is aware of their efforts, outside the communities in which they work. Again, there are, of course, the nationally recognized African-American reporters like Juan Williams who works for Fox News and Gwen Ifill of PBS. But there are also people out there who have been working for years like Cynthia Tucker of the Atlanta Journal-Constitution and Ellis Cose of Newsweek who have their own unique perspectives on black life and American life in general. Some black writers are more radical than other, less afraid to criticize the system than others; then there are others who are more a part of "the system" such as writer and commentator Armstrong Williams, who appears weekly on the America's Black Forum discussion group. He is to the right; Juan Williams is to the left; Ellis Cose might be seen as being in between politically. The point is that that there are different black perspectives being put out there for us to listen to, from the radical left to the conservative right and they all deserve a listen. But sometimes we must seek them out. I encourage you to discover who are the more prominent black journalists working out there in the world today, to identify them and then to consider conversing with them, whether in person, through letter, phone or e-mail, just to see where they might stand on some issues critical to your life. Journalists and writers are always filled with ideas—this is what they are paid for and you might find them having a wealth of suggestions for you on how to meet and greet everyday life. They might also describe to you how they deal with life professionally, everyday, in a white dominated world. They might also relate to you why you do not see more black faces or hear more black opinions circulated in the general media dialogue. Journalists, I know for a fact, are more willing to hear from the public more than most people, because public response and sentiment shapes whom they are and even gives them more ideas to write about; and I guarantee you that black journalists are always willing to discuss black issues. A collection of these issues poured into their laps and on their desks might inspire them with the hope that that there are people out there listening and searching for voices to champion their causes. A united black people might find the black media community to be its strongest ally. Tell the black journalists that you are listening to them, that you have opinions and that you respect theirs.

14. Attend A Church Service

I'm probably preaching to the proverbial choir on this one, as black people are perhaps more apt to attend church on a regular basis than any other indigenous, native group in America. It's in our blood and history, as traditional as anything else that single out our community for its distinctiveness. Black faith and loyalty to God in fact has been so strong in my lifetime, that I even considered for a moment that Heaven might be peopled mostly by African-American, when all is said and done. This is a silly thought and passed through my mind quickly; but the reality I see, the investment in worship among black Americans compared to whites across the country, seems to bear up the fact that blacks seem at least on the surface to be more faithful to the Protestant God of the bible—introduced to us generations ago by our slave owners—than the descendants of the slave owners themselves. Many of these people have forgotten God, chased him out of their hearts. With blacks for the most part, this does not seem to have been so. All this is personal observation, from someone who has lived on both coasts and in the middle of the country for a spell and been able to observe black worship in all three places; but I am not willing to say that blacks are stronger believers than whites, or any other ethnic group, because I have not attended churches representing other groups to any significant degrees. It's just a feeling I have that black people in general have a more deeply rooted respect for God's promises as given in the bible and a generational patience to wait them out. In this sense then, the black American is like the Children of Israel, in his generational faith. Unfortunately, however, even black piety seems to have declined over the years. Drugs, crime, broken families and a fractured, less cohesive community has sent us scurrying in various spiritual directions over the years, some in no direction at all. Many of us have given up completely, in many cases influenced by the general agnosticism and cultural relativity espoused today by the country at large. I don't have the numbers, but I would venture to say that if a poll were taken of blacks today, we would see perhaps the largest number of them declaring themselves as atheists in the history of black America, something that would be a remarkable development so soon after the post-Martin Luther King era. But again, I have not facts. This is just an intra-cultural hunch. Meanwhile, if not outright non-believers in the existence of God, many blacks are investigating other religions, particularly Islam, and particularly black males, who have lost hope more than most, with lives filled with prison, death, hate, fear, insecurity, low self-esteem and self-loathing. These people, black males like myself, are searching for something, anything, to give their often-brief lives some significance. Of all the different racial groups out there now inhabiting this great, vast land, it is the black male who has always occupied the frontlines of America's socio-cultural warfare. We have always been the first group to be sacrificed for America's prosperity. And unaware of our daily martyrdom, we toil on looking for answers. The plight of the black male is perhaps worse today than ever because there are many more ethnic groups in America now vying for some kind of control, pushing the black male further and further behind as he searches for identity and meaning to his life. This leads him to lead a life of desperation. Therefore, black males, young ones specifically, are perhaps—from my experience—the most absent in the congregation in the average Sunday morning church setting. In desperation and doubt they have turned their backs on God.

Well, I am here to tell all blacks that they should not give up on God. What we need to do is to continue to look at the big picture and not be ground down by the daily hardships of life, and I encourage older people, men and women, to reach out to the young and get them back into the church. This is crucial. Older black women in particular might be able to reach young black males, as such black males might be less threatened by the grandmotherly type. Black males are often threatened—from my experience—by other black males, young or old. And "young" women should not be used to go after black males, because black males might misconstrue the intent. The point is that there are ways to get black men into the church. It just might take some creativity, some will and a lot of prayer.

In general, I am encouraging here a trip to church for all black Americans, if nothing else, to share in a worship experience with those of your own kind. I guarantee that if you are open-minded and your spirit is willing, you will enjoy yourself, meet some kind people—not the cold, harsh sometimes disingenuous people you deal with regularly in the world—but some genuine folks who, hopefully, will have your best interest in mind. After leaving such a service, and after digesting whether your spirit and overall demeanor has improved, you might want to return. And if you do decide to return, I hope that you will make an effort to bring a black male along, because "we" need to be there the most, in my observation.

Lastly, am I suggesting a particular type of church, religion or denomination? Well, you will have to decide that for yourself, based on what I have said. But I will say this: let your spirit be your guide. For a moment, if you will, acknowledge the existence, power, wisdom and authority of an all mighty figure, get on your knees and speak to this figure for about 10 minutes or so and ask him which direction you should go. I guarantee you that, if your request is a sincere one, you will receive an answer or some prompting one way or the other. Where you should go and worship will be related to you. But you have to open your mind and spirit and listen.

13. Meet A Black Minister

Black ministers are strewn throughout your community, religious professionals waiting for you to visit and talk to them about life, about God, community, hope, fear, sorrow, depression, love, loss, family, children and government. You don't need to take a pill or talk to a counselor or therapist. Talk to your neighborhood minister during his or her office hours. They would be more than happy to discuss any range of issues with you. It's their job and for those afraid to make an appearance on Sunday mornings, meeting the minister in person might provide insight into the nature of his or her church before you even visit. Again, there are treasure troves of wisdom in the mind, soul and spirit of many black ministers across the nation, waiting to be explored. Lest we forget, these are men and women of God himself, people that have taken vows to represent God, so if they are in any way dishonest or disingenuous, they have to answer to a higher power. Therefore, the likelihood of such behavior from them is low. They are professed men and women of God and we should all feel comfortable putting our trust and concerns into their hands.

To make something like this happen, you would need to put yourself in touch with a church secretary or some person like that, and tell that person that you are a citizen of the neighborhood who may or may not have any church experience, but that you have some special concerns to discuss with the minister. You ought to be invited in with open arms. And you should not be afraid to discuss any subject, because the person you will be talking to will be a black person like you, perhaps older than yourself and more experienced in life than yourself but in possession of a unique and wise way of seeing the should that he or she would be willing to share with you to deal with your problems.

12. Smile More

The eyes are the windows of the soul and sometimes a smile can be phony, but it still helps to show your teeth one in a while to the world. Smiling frees something within you. I know. I have been accused of not smiling throughout my life, in photos, sometimes among family. But this was not because I was not happy. It was because I was kind of self conscious of the spacing of my teeth. You could tell that I was happy from my bright eyes or a grin on my face but rarely would you ever see my teeth. But over time, and today, I am not self-conscious anymore for the simple fact that my teeth are not nearly as bad as I thought they were. I show them more now and smiling makes me feel good, especially to strangers who are the last to expect it and I always smile to children; and from children, I have become good at getting a return smile. Simply stated, smiling makes me feel good.

I am not talking about some goofy smile plastered on your face for no reason or a phony smile, worse yet, but a genuine heart warming smile delivered at the right times, at the right places can light up an entire bus of people, an otherwise solemn group or occasion, a child or group of children or just someone on the street. But such smiles have to come from a good place within you to be effective. It is up to you to find this place.

My recommendation would be to first know the value of your smile and then to try it out at various times and situations. If you are shot down from time to time by a returning frown, do not be discouraged. You will become successful in stimulating someone else through your smile after some practice. I would suggest trying your smile on a child first, preferably an infant. They are easy to make smile and laugh and will make good practice for you, because the fact is that all of us, even adults, still possess that child-like way about us. And if we can get good at making young kids smile through our own smiles, then we can work our way up to adults. And lastly, we must remember that learning to emit a genuine smile is also good for our own well being. It can make us feel good. If you don't know how to smile, practice in a mirror or have someone look at you to see how you might be projecting yourself to the world. Remember to show your teeth, to work your face muscles into the right positions, and to open your eyes wide so that people can see that you mean what you are doing.

You can also practice smiling at people in the street to see what type of reaction you will get. No matter what the response, people will know that after seeing you and your teeth, that they might have just seen a genuinely happy and content individual.

11. Matter

Don't just stand on the sidelines in your life. In some way, some how, make your life matter. Make yourself matter in "a good way," of course, not through some cruel or bad act. But make yourself known, hopefully to the benefit of those of your own kind, other black people. You need to matter in life and this does not depend on your "station" in life. You can matter wherever you are, in big ways and small. You can matter by being a good father or mother, neighbor, friend, church member, patron or businessperson. The point is to spread your spirit among other people in positive ways. Try to be known for good things, such as helping others.

Sometimes, though, we are "forced" to matter. We are called to take on challenges and to fight as Dr. King was called in the 1960s. But we should always be ready to matter in our lives, because we never know how we might be called. The encouragement here is then twofold: live to matter and be ready to matter because you never know how you might one day affect the world at large or how life may affect you. In addition, you might never know how life might draw you out and call on you to integrate your mind, body and soul into humanity at large. Would you be ready to expose yourself? Would you be comfortable with yourself to matter to others? Do you think that you have something special to offer for the betterment of others? You need to ask yourself these questions, because the fact is that we "all" matter and affect others and the world at large to various degrees. But the encouragement here is matter "actively," for selfless reasons.

10. Mix It Up

Sometimes when we decide that we are going to "matter" in life we might be forced to mix it up with the forces out there that might disagree or even oppose what we have chosen to matter about. Whenever you take a stand there will always be those who will come up against you. Dr. King and Abraham Lincoln were examples of this in action. But this does not mean that we run and hide and not decide to matter. We just have to be unafraid to fight for what we believe in and not be afraid to "mix it up."

Mixing it up is a state of mind that you carry around with you, based on a will to fight for what you believe in. It does not necessarily mean mixing it up through violence or anything physical, though some of us might be pushed in this direction from time to time. I do not advocate violence. But mixing it up can mean, at the very least, raising your voice to the rafters when your principles and personal integrity come under assault. You always have a right to defend such principles through the spoken word.

Even out there in the world, when you disagree with something politically, or in the media, do not be afraid to write a letter in disagreement and "mix it up" with those in power, who in many cases take our will and desires for granted. In fact if you don't mix it up, you might find yourself one day bereft of the will, ability and right to get involved ever again. It is, therefore, always important to take a stand when we feel we have been aggrieved, because we never know: when we take that stand we might be doing so for hundreds, perhaps thousands of others who have not the will to "mix it up" like you do. I have no doubt that there are still some strong black people out there, men and women, who are unafraid to get out there and have their words heard and emotions felt. They just need to do it. Doing so might let the rest of the world know that the American black community is still powerful, still has a voice and a will to make a difference on a global scale.

9. Love

I don't have to tell anyone how to love. It is my sincere, deep belief in the human character that leads me to believe that we all still "really" know how to love one another. The problem is that many of us just don't want to make to effort or forge the will to do so. But all of us are born with and possess the innate instincts to love one another. I do not believe that we are naturally hateful creatures. All babies are born needing love for their complete development and if given it by parents, loved ones and society at large, babies are more than willing to return that love. I do not believe in the Bad Seed theory. What we must do is to generate that love for one another in ourselves and pour it out into society at large. Such an outflowing from individuals might affect society in waves like ripples in water. We must harness our instincts to love. To do this, to draw out these instincts, it would help us to find out what and who out there is in need of love. We could then use our love gifts to serve others. Again, children are good to practice on because they receive and give with so little effort and they need our affection very much for their own development. Your job then would be to discover how to best love your own child, if you have one. If not, discover how to best love a parent, relative or other loved one. Practice loving this individual and your natural propensity to love unconditionally—the ideal form—might be generated in you. Showing love for a child might come in spending time with he or she, helping with homework, playing a game or teaching something. Showing love for an adult might involve more complicated actions. But one thing it would involve, once that need for love has been identified, is patience. Don't give up on loving and attempting to love, even when things get rough. Perhaps, however, some of you might need to rediscover, or to discover for the first time, what *love* means. What is the definition of love? If this is so, I would encourage you to consult a dictionary first and then perhaps, a minister.

8. Listen

Not only do we live in a louder world but we live in a selfish one in which people only listen to one another selectively. We tend to listen only to the things that make us feel good, as we do not want to feel any discomfort whatsoever. What we need to do is listen, to the best of our abilities, to everyone about everything. Especially, we need to listen to those people and pay attention to those circumstances close to us and not selectively.

Do not be afraid to listen. Do not be afraid that what you hear might make you uncomfortable. It might. You might find yourself uncomfortable around people of a particular racial group and one night for example, you may find yourself in a movie theater surrounded by a particular group of these people speaking in its own unique language and acting out in its inimitable mannerisms that, from your previous experiences, you have decided that you do not like. Well, instead of changing seats to get away from this source of your discomfort, try listening to what these people are saying to get some insight into how their minds work and what is important to them. This might give you a means to communicate with this particular group of people in the future. This is if you have the will to do so. You might even, after to listening to this pre-film conversation, even engage in a conversation with the members of this group, a critical conversation that can make you all feel comfortable and satisfied with your night out on the town.

You need to listen. You need to listen to kids most of all. Give them your ear. Recognize their age after you have heard them so that you will know how to best respond. Adults can often say things that are superfluous, even silly and unimportant at times, but kids rarely say anything that has absolutely "no" meaning, something that might be important to note in their development. I'm not saying to tape record kids or listen outside the doors of their rooms. I'm just saying that where kids are concerned we should listen and be attentive to overall patterns and changes in their lives so we can be ready to be there when important decisions regarding their lives need to be made. If we have been listening to them all along, then we will be well informed when time comes to make those important decisions.

Open your ears. There are a world of sounds to hear. Sounds that make up life itself. One day, try even listening to the silence, or even go out into the woods and listen to nature itself. Listen to the birds, some rushing waters—if you are around them—winds blowing in the streets, the sound your foot makes when it cracks the twigs or gravel beneath your feet, your breathing as you try to scale a small hill. As black people, we need to listen outside the box. Such listening is informative and information, again, yields power.

7. Hope

Never give up hope. To do so would mean that you are no less than spiritually dead. Hope, like love, is built into the human character and hope has gotten us as a people extremely far in the world, perhaps to the point where we are today and hope will enable us to continue on to tomorrow. Hope is the engine of the spirit. But it needs to be revved up and excited from time to time. Once revved up, the foot needs to stay on the accelerator so that we can live in perpetually hopeful states.

It was hope that allowed Frederick Douglas to escape slavery and live the rest of his life as a free man; it was hope that allowed Harriet Tubman to also escape slavery and then to help others to escape on the Underground Railroad; it was hope that enabled Dr. Martin Luther King to lead a social movement that would lead to a change in the very fabric of American society. There is power in hope and the will. Hope can inspire and fuel the will to do something, whatever that thing may be, because with hope you do not depend on the things in this world that you see. Instead, you depend on the possibility for positive breakthroughs in your life that have nothing to do with this world. We as black people have come a long, long, long, long, long way on hope throughout the history of this country and there is no reason to stop now. The hopeless leave their fates to the whims of this world and what they see around them; the hopeful see and feel beneficence beyond and outside the things they can see and touch and feel.

6. Work

We all must work. We must do so because we all must survive and crime is not the answer. Yes, there are many black men in jail but many are there because they knew the difference between right and wrong and they chose wrong. There may not be many jobs or opportunities out there for them, but there are other ways to work and we should be humble enough to take jobs that we might think are beneath us. Not only does work give you some "legal" income but it can build self-esteem and feelings of self worth. A job, any job, can also lead to some things better. Once your job, whatever it is, has led to more responsible feelings in you and more confidence, you might want to expand and pursue other directions, responsibilities and careers. But you have to first begin somewhere and you should not be ashamed to take certain kinds of jobs. They can always lead to bigger things. I have a degree from college, but over the years, I have found myself working as a security guard and a cab driver while I tried to get my life back in balance and to pay the bills. Part of me wondered why I had come to be in those positions in my life, but I took them seriously and gave my best. I respected the jobs themselves and the duties I had to perform.

That was to address the people out there who think there is nothing out there for them to do. Next I would like to address those black people out there who have "good" jobs and still may not want to work. My response here is that we live in a lazy world now, with many conveniences and amid an unstated philosophy of "comfort at all costs." We cannot allow ourselves to become sucked into this mentality. We must continue to work hard and diligently to feed our families, as well as to feed our souls. Only after we have worked, putting forth our maximum efforts, can we relax. We must be willing to earn our comfort and not take it for granted or expect it with no effort. In the end, this can only lead to a weakening of values, personal stability and the strength of the black community as a whole. There is a tradition of hard, diligent work among our people, from the slaves on down. The American government has been kind enough to offer up to its poor welfare and other systems to keep us from poverty and suffering. We should be thankful for such programs, but we should also not take them for granted or take advantage of them. We should be more responsible. If we can work, then we should work and we should work hard, to get the job done, but not to excess, not to the detriment of health and family. A balance is always possible.

Lastly, I would address those young black males out there again, many of whom decry often the lack of jobs for them in the world. I would say to them that if you absolutely find it difficult to find substantial, fulfilling work, then why not just go to work for your family and loved ones. Not for money, but to help build them up and support them. This takes some responsibility and responsibility can begin anywhere, especially in the home. For example, do the shopping for your families, clean up the house, take your little brother or sister to school in the mornings. All these types of things build character in a young man or woman, character that might lead to eventually seeking out a job, getting that job and then moving on from there. It can be a chain reaction of responsibility, faith and hope, and all based in love.

5. Rest

After you have worked, you need to rest. There is no glory in over working yourself. There is only gluttony. Like you should not overeat, you should not overwork. The consequences are negative, either to health, family and relationships, not to mention peace of mind. And you have the right to rest and should not feel guilty about it. But you must earn it. It is not as satisfying, or even as relaxing, if it is not earned. Just like when we eat. We should, ideally, only eat to satisfy hunger and not just pour it on. We should earn our meals through work and we should earn our rest after work.

Try to rest your minds in addition to your bodies. I would recommend, if possible, a return to nature when possible. Perhaps a brief camping trip, where you could get away from the sights and sounds of your normal environment. Whatever you do, and whenever possible, take time to stop your mind from churning in the manner that it is used to. Allow yourself to relax, body, mind and soul.

4. Worship

Give something to something outside yourself. There is a tradition of worship in the world. Join in. Most of you already do worship and atheism is not an option. We live in a world that was created and only a being much, much, much greater than ourselves is capable of such creation and natural art. Our goals, our jobs, as individual creations, are to figure out the intentions of this great being. Why did he create the world and us in it? For what purpose? How does he feel about us now and how should we feel about this being?

Nature itself screams of a transcendent being. Acute, serious investigations of it reveal marvelous wonders that mankind has, incredibly and over time, foolishly come to take for granted. And the more we distance ourselves from nature, the more we disrespect it, the more we disrespect and distance ourselves from its creator. Nature is the unquestioned evidence of the work and existence of an all-powerful creator, it is my opinion.

If you believe me, then how should we address this individual? Well, there is only one testimony that gives us insight into his character, in addition to assigning him the status of creator. This is the Bible. The bible describes this individual called God in great detail, tells why we should worship him, when we should worship and how we should do it. It also tells us why the creator created all things and us: because he loves us and he asks us to worship him, because we are his children and he is our most benevolent father. He wishes only our good, and worshipping him is our agreement to follow the straight and good path that he has set before us.

There are of course, many other "religions" around the world that make similar and different claims of deity and call for various kinds of devotions. But only the God of the Bible reveals himself to man directly, describes himself and explains his reasons for creating the world; he is also the only being who claims that he created the entire world, saying that he did so not out of power or vanity but out of love for his creations.

Now the theme in this particular essay asks the reader, the black American, to simply worship. Worshipping calls on us to get outside of ourselves and give devotion to something that we consider greater than ourselves and worthy of respect and worship, with the hope that some benefits and rewards will come from our worship. Worship in itself is a good thing because it opens up a reverential side of our selves that keeps at bay, our more selfish natures. But truth is another thing and what the worshipper must ask himself, particularly if his or her needs are not met as he or she would like them, is if he or she through worship is pursuing the correct path to truth? Will there be either physical or spiritual manifestations of a particular brand of worship that an individual might be able to share with others? In other words, is the person on the path to truth as I say? You can worship a stone, or the sun, or a washing machine, or a hair dryer, but what is it that you are getting out of this worship and what is that you are ultimately seeking? You "should" be in it to better your life, to enlighten yourself to the meaning of ultimate "truth." If this is not your goal and there has been no satisfaction in your form of worship, then you might want to consider the value, direction and benefit of your particular brand of worship. Absolute truth should always be your ultimate goal. We live in a world now where absolute truth is in question, a world of relativity. But then I would ask you this: why worship at all in such a world? And if we eventually do not worship something greater than ourselves, then we might eventually begin to worship our own selves, each other, and what "we" ourselves have created. Such pursuits can only lead to a world of competing vanities and eventually to destruction. We, as people, must find sources of worship, and in that worship, seek the nature of absolute truth. Such absolute truths are already clearly found and can be seen in nature itself. Our jobs are to discover what, or whom, is behind nature's perfection.

3. Believe

Like we should make ourselves "matter" for something, we, as black people, also need to "believe" in something. Believing in something gives direction and purpose to our lives. And we all need direction and purpose in our lives. But what must we believe in? I cannot tell you what to believe in. But I can make suggestions. Again, I point to the search for ultimate, absolute truth. What is the source for all that I see and hear around me? Did it all evolve naturally, as science and some scientists would have us believe, or was there some direct purpose and intention behind it that we have to come to understand. We can believe various things, ideas, opinions and people from day to day, but would it not be beneficial to our lives if we could discover the "absolute" truth behind everything and then have this for us and our families to believe in? Undoubtedly.

What do you believe in? Are there things that you believe in that you cannot put into words and that you don't think about that often, yet they guide you through your daily lives? I don't know what these things might be, but you need to investigate, to break down the things you believe in to see if they make sense and if they are beneficial to your life. Or perhaps altering your belief structure might improve your life somehow. Do you believe, for example, that all people are basically good or basically bad? What makes you come to your conclusion one way or the other? You feel a certain way because you believe a certain thing or a certain way. Can you put those beliefs clearly into words and apply the values of your beliefs to your life and to the lives of others? What do you believe, how sincerely do you believe it and how much of what you believe comes directly from you and how much from influences outside yourself?

2. Have Faith

God here immediately comes to mind and yes this is my intention. Faith like hope can be a powerful motivator and sustainer. Faith can empower us and keep us moving along. Which God? This is up to you, of course. Some people discard God when it comes to faith. They might have faith, in other words, but it might not be in God. To this I would say that their "faith" is in fate, luck, probability or statistics, that somehow things and life might somehow bend in their favor if they just believe hard enough and live their lives a certain way. These people do not necessarily believe that there is a God out there in control of and orchestrating their fate. And he may not be, because we all have freewill to make the decisions that we want anyway. The difference with faith in a deity or all-powerful God, however, is that we turn over our critical, in fact, all life decisions to this deity, with the belief that he will take over things in our best interests.

1. Discover Your Reason For Living

Why are you here? At some point in your life you must ask yourself this question. There is always a cynical way out of all this. You can just say that you don't care why you are here. You are here and there is nothing you could have or can now, do about it, so why get philosophical? I would venture to say, in fact, that most people perhaps feel this way in the jaded world in which we live. But there must be a reason for your life. Number one, your life is not your own. Since your birth, it has not been because since you were born your life has affected and influenced the lives of others, so you could say that you have some responsibilities in your life and what you do with your life. You are not alone and you are not an island. No man is an island.

It would then behoove us all to discover our purposes in life. The earlier the better. The earlier we do it, the better chance of or achieving maximum impact and effectiveness with our lives. There can be no stepping aside, because if we do not assess our roles in the world as early as possible and consciously, then we run the risk of sliding into the tidal waves of public life and losing any control we might have. Public life would dictate our lives, in the absence of our abilities to make decisions for ourselves.

Personal destiny should begin in the home under the guidance of parents and siblings, all working together to discover one another's roles in the world, often beginning with simple questions during the early years, such as: what do you want to be when you grow up? Such activity in a broken home might not exist, therefore the child's dreams and assessment of his or her role in the world might be put on hold until later, or worse, perverted and corrupted to the point where the child ends up doing things he or she might have never done with the proper guidance. Early family life and foundations of life roles are essential to discovering who we are and our purposes for living. But then again, "the discovering of our purposes in life" might be a heavy-handed way of putting things. There is a hint of pressure there that does not have to be. No one should be forced to discover his reason for being born into such a vast universe. This is not necessarily our responsibility. Our goals are to recognize the impact that our individual lives might have on other people and the world at large and figure out if we want to use the gifts that we have for good—to improve matters that we affect—or negatively, making things worse, either consciously or not. Or perhaps we might just decide to keep moving along, paying no attention to the world or loved ones, only using the gifts we have been given for the betterment of our own selves. Such ethical considerations concerning our lives are essential to discovering our reasons for living, it is my belief. Were we sent here to help the world and others? Were we sent here to be burdens to the world? Or were we sent here to only to serve the self? Some people take years to discover this; some never do; some discover how they want to impact the world early; some just keep moving without such considerations. These are the critical questions concerning each and every life, it is my belief.

The point is that we all impact the world whether we like it or not. Our goals as black folks are to determine how we want to shape that impact, what we want to make our lives all about. And it's not about money, or having the most. Janitors impact the world positively or negatively, secretaries, truck drivers, housewives, presidents and congressman. So the point here again is not to discover the reason for living, but how we want to impact the world with the lives we have been given.

0-595-31439-2

www.ingramcontent.com/pod-product-compliance
Lightning Source LLC
Chambersburg PA
CBHW020239290526
45784CB00003B/1039